Table of Contents

CONTENTS

Parent's Guide to

PlayStation
Games

CONTENTS

Parent's Guide to
PlayStation
Games

AUTHOR

Author and journalist Craig Wessel has been writing in the eletronic entertainment industry for over five years. Craig came upon the idea for the *Parent's Guide* series while writing the strategy guide for the PC game *Kingpin*, one of the 30-plus titles he has in print. Craig joked that he had little to write about, since so much of the language in the game was too risqué to be transcribed into the book. The jokes led to curiosity about how the computer game ratings system worked, the quantity of information available to parents, and the accuracy of existing resources intended to help parents make educated choices. After a little research, Craig decided the best thing to do was write a book himself that would serve as a resource for parents. The result is the book you hold in your hand. Craig currently lives outside Dallas, with his wife Debbie and twins, Adyson and Evan.

AUTHOR'S ACKNOWLEDGEMENTS

This book (and series) is the result of many long hours of work by many people. My name may be on the cover, but this was definitely a team effort from start to finish.

First, I'd like to thank the Stratos Group - Zack Schiel, Matthew Rorie, and Brett Norton for their stupendous effort on this, and all three books in the series. The attention to detail and the sheer quantity of titles we were able to cover were a direct result of many hours of hard work by them. Be sure to check out their other game-related stuff at **www.stratosgroup.com.**

Of course, I have to thank Ed Steussy (Publisher, Mars Publishing) for what has become a rather successful collaboration. However, as Ed will attest, this book wouldn't be in your hands without the rest of the Mars Publishing team—Lars Peterson, Michael Duggan, John Voland, and Fabienne Vitiello. They burned the candle at both ends, and in the middle as well to get this project completed. Ready for the next one, guys?

Finally, my wife deserves a special mention as always, for putting up with the long hours it takes for me to indulge my hobby-turned-business. Without her support, none of this would be possible.

ACKNOWLEDGEMENTS

Parent's Guide to PlayStation Games

PUBLISHER'S ACKNOWLEDGEMENTS

No book is ever created in a vacuum, and the *Parent's Guide to Computer and Video Games* series certainly wasn't.

Our thanks go first and foremost to Dr. Arthur Pober and his team at the ESRB. Few people appreciate the difficulties involved with reviewing thousands of games and websites every year, organizing that data and maintaining the consistency and separation necessary to make their ratings the undisputed Gold Standard of the industry.

Doug Lowenstein and the IDSA have been instrumental in allowing us access to information and contacts which would have been difficult—if not impossible - for us reach in time to go to press. These books have achieved the standard they have due to their efforts.

Our thanks to PCData, for providing detailed information on game sales, so that we could pinpoint which ones needed to be included.

Everyone at Mars put out a special effort for the series—their names are recognized elsewhere in the book. Amy Yancey, Mars' long-time Production Manager, made important contributions early in the project before leaving to further her education. We wish her the very best of luck in her new pursuits.

Mars Publishing has made every effort to make sure that these books are error-free. If you spot any errors we have missed, or would like to offer suggestions in general, please forward them to **parentsguides@marspub.com** or to our Los Angeles office address.

ACKNOWLEDGEMENTS

Introduction

The Parent's Guide Series

When making the decision to publish this series of books, we were committed to helping parents stay informed about the games their children played. We knew that with thousands of titles in existence and hundreds more being released each year, even the most involved parent could use some help. However, our big concern was whether or not the market would support a three-book series of this nature. Given the concerns over the impact games have on our children, we were fairly certain that parents would appreciate some additional information on the subject, and our research revealed some interesting information that more than justified the Parent's Guide series.

> • In 1999, 215 million computer and video games were sold in the United States, making Interactive Games the fastest growing entertainment industry segment with sales of $6.1 billion . This does NOT include international sales.
> • Sixty percent, or roughly 145 million, of Americans over the age of six say they routinely play computer and/or video games.
> • Nearly half of computer and video game players are under 18, but a full 87% of purchasers are over the age of 18. Eighty-four percent of underage purchasers get a parent's permission before buying.
> • A resounding 83% of parents say they try to watch every game their kids play and 89% claim to be present when their children buy or rent a game.
> • For the third year in a row, more Americans said that playing interactive games was more fun than any other entertainment activity-a full 35% in 1999. Compare that to those who said television (18%), surfing the Internet (15 %), reading books (13%), going to the movies (11%), or renting movies (6%).*

Not only does there seem to be a thriving market and need for titles of this nature, but that demand is only growing. The Parent's Guide series is designed to cover the games available for each platform, and also give you as a parent some insight into an industry that is becoming increasingly influential.

*Courtesy of IDSA (Interactive Digital Software Association).

A Parent's Guide to PlayStation Games

There are two worlds in video games: the console world—which revolves around systems like the PlayStation, PlayStation 2, Nintendo 64, Dreamcast, and by extension the Nintendo Gameboy (which is basically a portable console)—and the world of Computers. The Parent's Guide series covers both the Personal Computer (PC) and the console world. Be sure to check out *A Parent's Guide to Computer Games*, and *A Parent's Guide to Nintendo Games* if your kids have a PC, Nintendo 64, or Gameboy.

This guide covers two of the most popular systems in the console world—the Sony PlayStation and the PlayStation 2. The PlayStation is Sony's workhorse—with over 900 games available in the U.S., it has the lion's share of the console market. The PlayStation 2 (PS2) was just recently introduced, and has already exceeded sales expectations, partially due to the fact that it is much more powerful, but also because it includes the ability to play DVDs as well as games.

Chapter 1: Sony

Here you'll find a historical overview of the company, its products and its philosophy.

Chapter 2: Platforms

This chapter will give you a quick overview of the different game systems, or platforms, available today. If you're still shopping for one, then this section is a must read. You'll find details about each platform, as well as some useful comparisons between them.

Chapter 3: Game Types and Genres

Before we dive into the games, you might need a few definitions if you're unfamiliar with game terms. You'll also find definitions of the common genres, or categories, that games are grouped into. From Action to Adventure and beyond, the second half of this chapter walks you through the various game genres you'll find on the shelves.

Chapter 4: ESRB Rating System

The ESRB rates video games and websites, much as the MPAA rates movies. A very important system for you to understand, and we've got it covered. With details about each rating, and the various descriptors you'll find on all game packaging, you'll be armed to make intelligent decisions about what games you bring home. We've also included an interview with Dr. Arthur Pober, founder and President of the ESRB, which provides an inside look at the rating system and the group that administers it.

Chapter 5: The Games

We've pulled together some information briefs that will tell you what you need to know about the hottest PlayStation and PlayStation 2 titles, including ratings and other important info about each title.

Closing the Gap

If you grew up during the 1970s or early '80s, then you were most likely affected, directly or indirectly, by video games. Beginning with their introduction into video arcades, and continuing with the first home entertainment systems (remember *Pong* or *Missile Command?*), video games have become commonplace in the everyday lives of children.

Computer games, and the massive influence of the Internet, have fostered an explosion in the popularity of video games. In recent years, much of the press that video games have received has been negative. We see violent kids, murderers even, who spend hour after hour playing violent games, and the assumption is made that violent games are at least partially to blame.

Making an assumption without good information to back it up isn't the wisest choice. Experts' opinions aside, the assumption that all video games are bad does nothing to help parents decide what to do when their child wants a certain game. A knee-jerk reaction of saying "NO!" to all games is not the best answer. Several games reviewed in these guides provide educational insights which might not be possible in a classroom setting. But given the variety of games available today, it's also not appropriate to assume that everything out there is good either, or that children are able to make good choices on their own.

This book isn't going to make the decision about which games your child should or shouldn't play for you, nor is it designed to provide ammunition to either side in the "Video Games: Good or Bad?" battle. What it is designed to do is provide you, the parent, with information about current computer and video games so that you'll be able to make an informed decision about what's right for your child.

Every child is different, as is every parent. Use this book as a resource to increase your awareness of today's games, and both you and your child will be better for it.

In the Beginning...

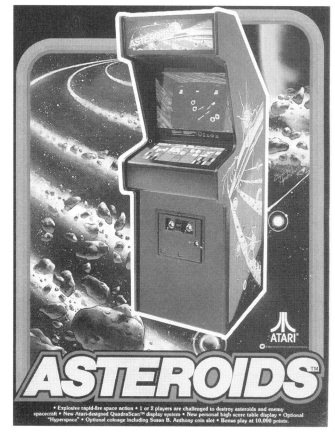

In the mid-1970s, video games were an anomaly. Found mostly in arcades and convenience stores, they were background noise that most parents tolerated. Many of the earlier games electronically re-created, either directly or by imitation, other games: sports, board games, and so forth. Developers of these early games built simple products that enticed kids to plunk quarter after quarter into them.

With their rise in popularity in the late 1970s and early 1980s, and the increasing variety of games available, video game arcades became "the" place for under-aged youth to hang out with friends. Not all of them played the games, but it's a given that, in some way, most were influenced by the social interaction that developed around them. It's quite likely that, if you weren't playing the games back then, you might have been doing something else at the arcade; after all, most of your friends were there doing the same things. For the most part, parents saw the arcade games themselves as harmless entertainment, and lamented the waste of money more than they worried about the actual content of the games.

Video Games vs. Computer Games

The term "Video Game" has come to refer to games made for any console (PlayStation, PlayStation 2, Nintendo 64, Gameboy, etc.). Games created for PCs are usually called "Computer Games" or "PC Games." Stand-alone games (such as those in arcades) are called "Arcade Games."

During this time period, video game manufacturers began creating home versions of popular games. Atari is a name you likely remember from this period, and for good reason. Following the release in the arcades of *Pong* in 1972, and its release as a separate game system in 1977, Atari subsequently created the Atari 2600— without question the most influential game system of its time. Hundreds of video games (over 1600 eventually) were created for the Atari 2600 console, and it spawned a new era in video gaming— video games as home entertainment. In the pre-VCR era, the video game console (as Atari-like systems came to be known) was one of the first devices to use the television to display content other than network broadcast programming.

Introduction

Virtual Reality?

Aside from the rise of the Internet, the most stunning changes since the '70s have been in the graphics area of video games. Gone are the days of grainy, blocky images that bear no resemblance to reality as we know it. Instead, today's games make full use of powerful graphics processors to render scenes in near-realistic detail. To see images that are the quality of current motion pictures, a computer would need to render approximately 80 million polygons, or geometric shapes, per frame. Translated to real-time action, with the player as actor, director, and producer, this would require rendering 24-30 frames per second, or roughly two billion polygons per second.

At present, the PlayStation 2 is the most powerful console, capable of rendering 66 million polygons per second, nearly the visual quality of the 1995 computer-animated film *Toy Story*, in real time. While we're a long way from the processing power needed to boost this capability to the two billion-polygon level, advances in processors are increasing exponentially. Many experts agree that sometime in this decade, the ability to create real time movie-quality games will exist. At that point, it will be a new ball game, with the very real possibility of movies created without physical actors. Also interesting is the possibility of movies created with digital images of real actors of past and present. Imagine Humphrey Bogart and Bruce Willis starring in a movie together, with Bogey performing lines he never said while alive, and absolutely no visual difference between reality and what you see on-screen, and you begin to get the idea.

This kind of technology is around the corner, but at present, games already exist that push the envelope and blur the line between reality and the digital world. We are approaching a time where playing a game will feel exactly like performing the same actions in real life. We're not nearly there yet, but the application of this sort of technology outside of games is promising. Uses in medicine, manufacturing, design, training, communications—all these and more will be impacted by the increase in rendering technology—a field that is being supported, and even driven forward, by games.

Chapter 1

Sony

Sony has long been associated with the consumer electronics field, creating a high-profile brand name while manufacturing products such as televisions, computer monitors, and audio devices. Even with this track record within the industry, few people thought the launch of their PlayStation home entertainment console would bring them much success. Earlier in the 1990s, much-hyped systems from companies like 3DO, NEC, and even the console veteran Atari had failed in the Sega and Nintendo-dominated console market. Given these products' unfortunate ends, and the relative stranglehold that the Nintendo and Sega systems had on the marketplace, the PlayStation looked like it would probably misfire as so many others had done.

The PlayStation quickly proved to be in the right place at the right time, however. Powered by a slick, multi-million dollar ad campaign, a strong lineup of games, and the fact that the system itself was simply well-designed and more powerful than the competition, the PlayStation has become the most successful console of the '90s, selling more than 70 million units worldwide, with almost 30 million of these being sold in North America alone. In the six years since its original Japanese release, over 4,000 software titles have become available for the system worldwide.

Though the PlayStation has been around for over half a decade, it shows few signs of slowing down. Despite pressure from rivals Nintendo and Sega, each of which have debuted new systems since the PlayStation's launch, the Sony console has consistently had the highest-selling games, with strong original titles and an impressive line of third-party games. Among the most popular titles are the *Final Fantasy* series of RPGs, the skateboard game *Tony Hawk: Pro Skater*, and the platform games featuring the console's most prominent mascot, *Crash Bandicoot*.

Sony has not been resting on its laurels, however. The PlayStation 2 console has recently shipped to stores across the country. Boasting a 300 MHz central processor and a DVD drive, this console will soon feature optional accessories like a modem and digital camera attachment. With at least a year before any more major entries into the console gaming market, Sony is placing itself in a strong position to continue its domination of the video game scene.

A Brief History of Sony's PlayStation

Considering the long odds against it, the PlayStation videogame console that Japanese giant Sony Corp. loosed upon the world in 1994-95 might've been a success even if it broke even. The console (known in the industry as the PSX) wound up outselling Nintendo's vaunted N64 console in Japan in 1994 and would, as of August 1998, sell more than 40 million units. Not even the most optimistic Sony executive had considered all of this success likely.

There were a number of impediments to the PSX's success. First, Sony was considered an audio/video company, not a computer or game company; second, Sony had little or no experience in the games business; and third, it was attempting to enter an industry largely controlled by Japan's most profitable company, Nintendo.

Not that Sony was any young stripling in the Japanese corporate forest. Sony CEO/cofounder Akio Morita had built the company out of the rubble of post-World War Two Japan with inspired decisions, followed by first-rate engineering and a marketing flair that no other electronics company possessed. First audio tape recorders, then transistor radios, then TV tubes, then VCRs, then the Walkman—through it all Sony changed all the rules of how Japanese corporations were supposed to behave.

Nintendo, on the other hand, was the epitome of the Japanese corporation. It was wildly profitable, yes, but also very internalized, very "vertical" in the sense that it preferred to dictate who supplied it and whom it in turn supplied. It was also very centralized; all decisions were made from the company's corporate headquarters in Kyoto.

The road to PlayStation began, as it happened, under Nintendo's aegis. In 1989, "The Big N" wanted a hardware partner that was experienced with CD-ROM drives, and Sony—having co-created the format with Dutch behemoth Philips NV years before—was the perfect choice, even though the two giants had never collaborated before.

What Nintendo wanted was the multimedia expertise Sony possessed to get the CD-ROM drive destined for its Super NES game console to perform as well as possible, and also to coordinate its audio and video synchronization. What Sony wanted was to get its corporate foot into Nintendo's domain.

Both parties were happy with the union initially. Nintendo got specs for its new CD-ROM drive that surpassed its expectations, and Sony placed an audio chip on the Nintendo SNES machines for which it retained all future development rights. What Nintendo didn't know was that Sony was intending to use that chip—as well as the new CD-ROM drive—on its own multimedia machine, the Play Station (space intended), a machine that would not only play music and game CDs, but would also have a port for Nintendo SNES cartridges. In other words, a Nintendo-killer.

By June of 1991, Sony's plans were laid and ready. At the summer Consumer Electronics Show in Chicago, Sony announced the development of the Play Station one day; then Nintendo, in a breath-taking bit of double treachery, announced that it had chosen Philips, Sony's longtime nemesis, to partner with Nintendo on the SNES CD-ROM drives.

Sony could have sued; it did not. Sony could have invoked the unwritten law among Japanese corporations—that none of them would ever turn down a Japanese company to work with a foreign one, no matter the circumstances.

Sony tried to get its revamped PlayStation, now without the space in the name and without the Nintendo SNES port, going again. The PSX was going to be a game machine, Sony had decided, to beat all game machines, especially Nintendo's SNES. Furthermore, it was going to include 3D acceleration, a first for a gaming machine. 3D video accelerators were just then, in 1993, starting to show up in the fastest home computers, but wouldn't be readily available for years yet.

Sony knew hardware like few others in the world; hardware was certainly not the problem for the PSX. But Morita and Ken Kutagari, who then headed up the PSX development team, acknowledged that software would indeed be the big problem; Sony was not then nor ever had been a software developer. Sony executives rounded up some 250 of Japan's leading software developers—including some of arcade gaming's leading lights, like Namco and Konami —- and set them loose with PSX developer kits. During development of the PSX, Sony focused on sleek appearance and total control for the player—factors Kutagari had insisted upon from the beginning of the PSX's design.

The stage was set for the PSX's Japanese launch, on 3 December 1994—just one week after the debut of Sega's latest console, the Saturn. The PSX sold 300,000 units in the first month, and went on to sell a million in Japan by the time the console was released in the U.S. market (9 September 1995). As it had in Japan and would do in Europe the following December, Sony's new baby was given a rousing reception—and Nintendo would never own the videogame market all by itself again.

And if anything, the PlayStation 2, already out in Japan and due out in the U.S. soon after this book goes to press, will further cement Sony's position. With its advanced DVD-capable drive, its computer-like processing power, and its wide network of software developers, the PS2 will carry the Sony name into the 21st Century as flagship of a newborn game console empire.

Chapter 2

Game Platforms

In game terminology, a platform is nothing more than the hardware a particular game is made for. Personal Computers, PlayStation, Nintendo 64—these are all platforms, and games can be created for each of them. In some cases, certain games are only made for one platform. However, in recent years, the trend has been to "port" or create versions of the same game for multiple platforms. As a result, the choice is no longer, "Which platform has the most games available?" but rather, "Which platform suits our needs?" As you'll see, this section gives you some general information on the most popular platforms that will help you make a decision. Even if you've already selected a platform, take a quick look through the information here—you may find something you didn't know about your purchase.

PlayStation and PlayStation 2
> The essentials on Sony's workhorse, the PlayStation, and its successor, the PlayStation 2.

Nintendo 64 and Game Boy
> Nintendo waded into Sony's market with a bang with the Nintendo 64, and their Game Boy sales are stronger than ever. Get the scoop on both in this section.

Dreamcast
> One of the newer console systems on the market, the Dreamcast boasts some of the most impressive processing power available. Can it hold its own against the newer PlayStation 2?

PC (Windows and Macintosh)
> A brief overview of the PC platform, along with some information about both Windows and Macintosh as separate game platforms.

Future Platforms
> Microsoft's X-Box and Nintendo's GameCube are yet to be released as of this writing. Take a look here to get some early info on these hot new game platforms.

Platform comparisons
> Which platform makes sense for you? Should you own more than one? Check out this section for some useful comparisons between all platforms.

PlayStation and PlayStation 2

Sony's PlayStation has long been the front-runner in the video games race. It's a stable platform, and due to its longevity, features, and the low cost of games made for the platform, it's the most popular console on the market. Given its strong market share and acceptance, the PlayStation has generated confidence in game developers and publishers, resulting in an enormous amount of games ported to this console. To date, there are over 900 games available in the U.S. for the Sony PlayStation.

Console

In general, the term "console" refers to any game system that is not a PC. Console systems are typically connected to the user's television, and they exist as separate pieces of hardware. PlayStation, PlayStation 2, and Nintendo 64 are all console systems.

Sony's Game Revolution

With sales of $19.1 billion in the U.S., and over $60 billion worldwide, Sony is a multimedia giant that has few peers. With their heavy involvement in co-developing the CD and DVD, as well as their role as a leading motion picture and television producer and distributor, it was inevitable that Sony would take a leading role in the electronic entertainment industry. Although it represents an admittedly small portion (roughly 10%) of Sony's revenues—over 60% of Sony's revenues are from the Electronics division—Sony Computer Entertainment is growing exponentially.

By the end of March 2000, shipments of PlayStation consoles numbered nearly 73 million units worldwide, with over 27 million sold in the U.S. alone. Put into perspective, nearly 10% of the U.S. population owns a PlayStation. With the introduction of the PlayStation 2, Sony is poised to smash PlayStation sales numbers—over 2 million PlayStation 2 units were sold during the system's first three months in the market.

With such a large volume of titles available, and with firm control of the console market, Sony's position was still anything but secure. With the Nintendo 64 and Dreamcast systems on the market, Sony faced a real threat, because the PlayStation's technology is outdated by today's standards—both the Nintendo 64 and Dreamcast boast more powerful processors and graphics capabilities. As a result, Sony unveiled what is currently the most powerful game platform on the planet, rivaling in some cases, the venerable PC—the PlayStation 2.

The PlayStation 2 is more than a game machine. It boasts the ability to play both CDs and DVDs as well, making it a complete entertainment device, clearly Sony's intent. If you choose, it is entirely possible to forget about purchasing a separate CD or DVD player, since a PlayStation 2 will offer you both, along with its game playing ability. Aside from its impressive technical specifications, this dual functionality is one of the features that is sure to keep the platform in the lead for some time.

For players, one of the most important features of the PlayStation 2 is that it is backward-compatible with other PlayStation titles. This means that as soon as the new system hits the streets, there will be over 900 games that will work on it.

PlayStation on the PC?

It's true in most cases that imitation is the highest form of flattery. However, Sony has taken a dim view of PlayStation emulators, in particular, a PC product called Bleem! which allows gamers to play PlayStation CDs on their computers instead of on the PlayStation console. Boasting improved 3D accelerated graphics for many titles, and consistent performance emulation of the actual console, Bleem! and other emulators insist that they are good for Sony's business, since they encourage ownership of PlayStation games.

Sony has disagreed vehemently, filing suit in several cases to block this type of action. Given the introduction of the PlayStation 2 and its advanced feature set, it's obvious that Sony has plans to chip away at the computer market, so any emulator that doesn't require a Sony console will likely be seen as a threat. To date, Sony has been unsuccessful in blocking emulator sales, resulting in substantial sales of these products.

Software Piracy & the IDSA

Software piracy is the illegal copying and/or counterfeiting of any computer software. This crime is unfortunately fairly widespread in the electronic entertainment industry, and is committed by young and old alike. Billions of dollars are lost annually due to pirated software, resulting in higher consumer costs and decreased tax revenues from sales tax. The IDSA (Interactive Digital Software Association), formed in April 1994, is designed to combat entertainment software piracy both in the U.S. and around the world. They estimate that worldwide piracy cost the U.S. entertainment software industry over $3 billion in 1998 alone. The IDSA provides policy work, education, and works in conjunction with U.S. Customs and other law enforcement personnel. The IDSA enforcement program is completely funded by dues from its members, a group that includes major software publishers worldwide. If you are aware of any entertainment software piracy, you can report it to the IDSA by email at **piracy@idsa.com**.

Unfortunately, the use of CD-ROM "copiers" and other simple programs that subvert publishers' copy-protection schemes has become acceptable to large numbers of otherwise law-abiding people. Internet message boards and newsgroups teem with information about where to obtain such programs, often for free or virtually so, and seek to justify their actions by blasting publishers' sales policies or proclaiming the freedom of the Internet.

Additionally there exist illegally copied or pirated software, mostly games, known as "warez," that are sold or otherwise distributed largely over the Internet. Whole Websites are devoted to the distribution of warez (rhymes with shares), but there is nothing legitimate or legal about them.

We strongly suggest that, if you notice your child playing a large number of new games without having paid for them, ask him or her where they came from.

PlayStation Classic

Although it's the older version of the newer and more feature-rich PlayStation 2, the PlayStation (or PlayStation Classic) is still an excellent choice. With a lower price point, it's a steal if you don't need to play the PlayStation 2's games. What's more, with over 900 games available—games that were made for the platform—you're not likely to run out of game choices anytime soon. In addition, there are still titles in development for the PlayStation. Of course, this will change over time, but in the interim, the PlayStation is a bargain.

Although the PlayStation 2 is now the king of the hill in the console market, Sony still has plans to support the PlayStation Classic. Along with the dozens of games still in development for the system, they have released a new, smaller PlayStation for the holiday season of 2000. The PS One, as it's called, is essentially a replica of the PlayStation, but smaller—nearly one-third of the original size. It's more portable than the original PlayStation, but it is not a hand-held system. It cannot run on batteries, nor is there a display screen to run PlayStation games on the go (though a small LCD screen will be available soon). Sony plans to eventually cease production of the original PlayStation design, with the PS One being the only available version of the PlayStation. The PS One doesn't feature any added capabilities, though, so any games released after the PS One's launch will still be playable on older-model PlayStations.

PlayStation Classic Technical Specifications

Here are the key features of the PlayStation console. Feel free to skip this section if, like me, you care more about the number of available titles and gameplay than you do about what's under the hood.

- Multiple independent custom processors with a 32-bit RISC CPU
- CD-ROM drive
- 2 controller ports, 2 Memory Card slots
- Renders up to 360,000 polygons per second
- Full-frame video at 30 frames per second
- 360-degree camera movement
- CD-quality sound
- Digital lighting and texture mapping capabilities
- Displays 16.8 million colors simultaneously
- Dual Shock Analog controller

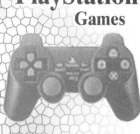

Control

The PlayStation originally shipped with a standard controller, but has recently included a Dual Shock Analog controller. Both feature the same basic buttons, but the Dual Shock Analog controller also includes two analog "joysticks" that enhance the player's control. The Analog nature of the controller means that it senses how hard you are pressing the buttons, adding another dimension to play. In addition, the Dual Shock controller gives the player feedback in the form of a vibration. Shoot something on-screen, make a tight turn in a racing car, or take a punch in a fighting game, and you feel it in the controller. This is a great enhancement to most games, so it's no wonder that Sony began shipping it as standard equipment.

Additional Products

When you buy a PlayStation, you get the console itself, as well as one Dual Shock Analog Controller, the power cord, and the A/V cable that connects the system to your television. In addition to this basic set-up, there are a number of additional accessories that you can purchase to add to your system.

Dual Shock Analog Controller—In addition to the one that ships with your PlayStation, you can purchase additional controllers to allow multiple players to play at once. If you want more than two players to play, you'll also need the Multiplayer Adapter mentioned later.

Memory Card—The Memory Card plugs into the controller and allows the user to save games. Although this is an accessory, it's a necessity for many games. Saved games can be resumed at a later time at the spot where you left off, even on another PlayStation.

Multiplayer Adapter—The PlayStation only has slots for two controllers. However, this handy accessory allows you to plug up to four controllers into one PlayStation to be used at the same time. This is the best way to avoid heated arguments if you have more than two kids.

PlayStation Link Cable—This is not as popular as the Multiplayer Adapter, simply because not many games support it. The Link Cable allows you to link two PlayStations, so that the same game is viewed (from each player's perspective) on two televisions. It works like those racing games you might have seen in arcades where more than one player can race another, but they are all on separate machines.

RF Adapter—This allows you to hook up your PlayStation to an older television that doesn't have the A/V input terminals needed to connect the console normally. Most consumers, even those without a newer TV, will have a VCR with the proper RCA inputs to run the PlayStation with the default cables, so be sure you really need the RF Adapter before purchasing it.

Steering Wheel—The Racing Wheel plugs into the PlayStation, and with the included pedals, completes the perfect console racing set up.

PlayStation 2

The second generation of the PlayStation, the PlayStation 2, is not only designed to be the ultimate game platform, but also to provide entertainment functions by incorporating a DVD player and a CD player. At the time of this writing, the PlayStation 2 is the most powerful console platform on the market, and many of the games in development for it are simply amazing. If you don't own a PlayStation, consider buying a PlayStation 2. As a bonus, you'll get a CD/DVD player, plus all the PlayStation titles will work with the PlayStation 2!

Technical Specifications

The features of the PlayStation 2 are impressive; at least, they are if you understand them. In simple terms, the PlayStation 2 is more like a computer than it is anything else. Much of its design incorporates features found only in computers up to this point.

- Supports Audio CD, DVD, and PlayStation discs.
- 2 controller ports, 2 Memory Card slots, 1 Optical Digital output, 2 USB (Universal Serial Bus) ports, 1 i-Link port, PC Card interface (Type III).
- CPU: Complete 128-bit Emotion Engine System Clock- 300MHz with 16KB cache memory. The PlayStation's CPU is only 33.8MHz.
- 32MB memory
- 20 million - 75 million polygons per second. For comparison purposes, the PlayStation only renders 360,000 polygons per second.
- CD Quality audio, plus software programmable voices.

Control

The PlayStation 2 ships with a PlayStation 2 controller that is nearly identical to the Dual Shock Analog Controller that ships with the PlayStation. The main difference is in an improvement within the control. Users report that the PlayStation 2 controller feels more responsive (however, this may be just a reflection of the overall improved feel of play on the new console). PlayStation controls will NOT work with the PlayStation 2.

Additional Products

At this time, there are only a few additional accessories available for the PlayStation 2, but over time, the same ones that are available for the PlayStation should become available.

PlayStation Dual Shock 2 Controller—This is the same controller that ships with the PlayStation 2 console, but you'll need more than one if you plan on playing multiplayer games.

Memory Card—PlayStation 2 Memory Cards hold 8MB worth of saved games, allowing you to save your game and return to it later, even on another PlayStation 2.

RFU Adapter—The RFU Adapter is used to connect a PlayStation 2 console to a television that does not have the A/V inputs normally required. Most new televisions are equipped with the A/V inputs; if you have an older television, the RFU Adapter will allow you to connect. Again, check your VCR for these inputs before you purchase an RFU adapter; most modern VCRs have the required inputs (small red, yellow, and white plugs).

S-Video Cable—If your television has an S-Video input, then you can purchase this accessory to provide better clarity compared to the regular A/V cable, or an RFU Adapter.

PS2 DVD Wireless Remote Control—This DVD Master Remote allows you to control the DVD or CD functions of the PlayStation 2 without using a connected controller. It features 16 function keys, and operates up to 23 feet away from the console.

Nintendo 64 and Game Boy

Chapter 2 • Game Platforms

Nintendo is no stranger to the electronic entertainment industry. After dominating the industry with the original Nintendo systems (NES and Super NES)—two of the new generation of home entertainment systems—Sony's introduction of the PlayStation was a serious threat to Nintendo's market share.

Nintendo

Nintendo is the grandfather of the console gaming industry. Starting as a Japanese playing-card manufacturer in 1889, the company first made an impact on American shores with the release of the Nintendo Entertainment System (NES) in 1985. With colorful, iconic games like *The Mario Bros., The Legend of Zelda, Donkey Kong*, and *Metroid*, the system was a huge success, establishing a foothold in America for Nintendo that the company still enjoys today.

The next pivotal system from the company was the revolutionary Game Boy, a hand-held, battery-operated gaming system. The Game Boy, with its fully-compatible descendent the Game Boy Color, have combined to sell over 100 million units around the world, more than any other electronic entertainment system in history. The original Game Boy system is still wildly popular, with new games being created for it even today, over a decade since its launch.

Building on the success of the NES, Nintendo released the aptly titled Super Nintendo in 1991. With advanced graphics and a wide array of games, the Super Nintendo was every bit as popular as its predecessor. The system carried on the tradition of the NES, with many of the game series that began on that platform continuing on with sequels for the Super Nintendo.

No company is perfect, and Nintendo is no exception. The greatest misfire in Nintendo's history occurred with the release of the Virtual Boy, a semi-portable gaming system that attempted to create a higher sense of immersion by utilizing two smaller screens inside a binocular-type viewer. While the sense of depth was somewhat impressive, the technical limitations of the hardware, which restricted the color of games to varying shades of red, proved to be too big of a hurdle, and no more than a handful of games were ever released for this now-defunct platform.

Nintendo rebounded with the debut of the Nintendo 64 in 1996. With support from their now-classic series of games, and a few new faces, the N64 has proven to be very popular in both Japan and America. Titles like *007 Goldeneye, Super Mario 64*, and *The Legend of Zelda: The Ocarina of Time* have propelled sales of the system to over 25 million units worldwide.

In the years since the launch of the Nintendo 64, Nintendo has maintained interest in the system, along with the Game Boy Color, by capitalizing on the popularity of its Pokémon property. If you have any younger kids, you'll likely be quite familiar with the Pokémon phenomenon. Dozens of N64 and Game Boy games have been created that are based on the adventures of these pocket monsters and their masters, sales of which, combined with peripheral products like trading cards and movies, are expected to reach $3 billion in the year 2000. The popularity of Pokémon has not begun to wane, and Nintendo is sure to continue to release products based on this property in the future.

Nintendo 64 (N64)

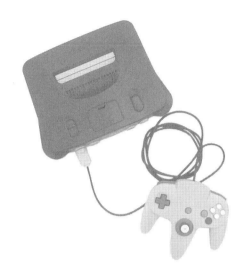

Built to compete with Sony's PlayStation Classic, the second-to-market Nintendo 64 is one of the most popular console systems on the market today. At its introduction, the Nintendo 64 (or N64 as it is commonly referred to) was the most powerful console on the planet, boasting unsurpassed graphics and CD-quality sound at a whopping (at that time) 93.75MHz. Add to that superior rendering ability, and you've got a platform that quickly outpaced the PlayStation Classic in nearly every category.

However, fewer titles have been created for the Nintendo 64, and the game cartridges tend to be more expensive than their PlayStation counterparts. Still, for those gamers who care more about graphics than the number of titles available, the Nintendo 64 has become the platform of choice.

Both the Dreamcast and PlayStation 2 now boast better graphics capabilities, but at a price point under $100, the Nintendo 64 is still a hot seller.

Nintendo 64 Technical Specifications

- 93.75MHz MIPS 64-bit RISC CPU (customized R4000 series)
- 36 Mbit RAMBUS D-RAM 36M bit memory
- 62.5 MHz RCP sound and graphics processor
- 32-bit RGBA pixel color frame buffer support
- 21-bit color video output

GRAPHICS PROCESSING:

- Z buffer
- Anti-aliasing
- Realistic texture mapping:
- Tri-linear filtered MIP-map interpolation
- Perspective correction
- Environment mapping

Nintendo 64 = Kid Friendly?

The perception in the video game market is that in comparison to Sony's PlayStation, games for the Nintendo 64 have been much more kid and/or family focused. How accurate is this perception? Well, there are over 900 titles available for PlayStation platform, compared to 248 for the N64. However, the percentage of titles given a "M" or Mature rating by the ESRB is only slightly higher for the PlayStation.

Only 21 out of 248 Nintendo 64 titles (8%) are rated "M", in comparison to 89 out of 955 (9%) for the PlayStation. Nintendo has made efforts in recent months to add more Teen and Mature games to its product line to tap a more adult market, but it's obvious that while there are certainly more "M-rated" PlayStation games, both consoles are clearly more heavily focused on Teen and family-oriented programming than their computer counterparts.

Control

The Nintendo 64's controller offers the option of using either buttons or the analog control stick to control the action. Its symmetrical design allows comfortable use by either left or right-handed players, and the expansion slot allows for insertion of memory modules or the optional Rumble Pack which allows players to feel the action as well as see it on screen.

Additional Products

In addition to the single controller that ships with the Nintendo 64 system, there are several additional components that can be purchased separately. These may or may not be affiliated with Nintendo.

 Funtastic Controllers—Identical in function to standard controllers, these controllers come in vibrant colors and are designed to add on to the N64 system to allow multiplayer action.

N64 Ultra Racer 64— The hand-held mini steering wheel for the N64 allows players to zigzag with the best of them for real control in racing games.

 N64 Powerpad—The ideal replacement or add-on controller; this is the same controller that ships with the N64 system.

 N64 Turbo Ram—Upgrades the N64 system to 8mb of RAM. More RAM = faster frame rates and more detailed graphics.

 N64 V3 Racing Wheel—With its separate foot pedals and Analog 300-degree wheel rotation, the N64 V3 Racing Wheel is a racer's dream.

 N64 Rumble Pack—Provides tactile feedback and lets players feel every bump, blow, or shot in Rumble Pack enabled games.

 N64 Gameshark—Plug this cartridge into the N64 to access hidden characters, levels, and cheats for Nintendo games. But bear in mind: Nintendo does NOT support this product.

Game Boy Color

The Game Boy has in many ways been a hotter property for Nintendo than the N64. Allowing players to take their games with them, the Game Boy has evolved into the Game Boy Color—a sleek, convenient way for Nintendo to re-market many games in a less-expensive (and infinitely more kid-sized) format. Boasting faster performance speeds than the regular Game Boy and a 52-color palette (32,000 colors), the Game Boy Color owns the hand-held video game market.

Originally, the Game Boy was an LCD product that could only render in black and gray. With the introduction of the Game Boy Color, sales and title licenses for the platform have skyrocketed. In addition, the Game Boy Color has allowed Nintendo to "colorize" 450 older Game Boy titles, resulting in additional sales on basically the same product. Given the nature of the platform, games for the Game Boy and Game Boy Color are consistently rated "E (Everyone)" and "T (Teen)" by the ESRB.

Technical Specifications

- 52 simultaneous color display
- Twice as fast as regular Game Boy
- Transforms 450 existing Game Boy games into color
- 32,000 colors available for new Game Boy Color games
- Compatible with the Game Boy Camera, Printer, and other accessories.

Control (Game Boy and Game Boy Color)

The Game Boy is an all-in-one product. The handheld console includes the control pad, LCD viewing screen, and a Select and Start button. The Game Boy doesn't allow the depth of control customization possible with the Nintendo 64, but games made for the platform usually don't require more than basic controls.

Additional Products

In addition to availability in a rainbow of colors, the Game Boy is also compatible with a number of products that enhance its functionality.

 Car Adapter—Fits car/boat lighter socket. Comes with 10-foot cord, allowing you to keep your Game Boy or Game Boy Color going on the road.

 Game Boy Pulse Pack—Attaches to the bottom of a Game Boy system and adds jolt/rumble effects during the gameplay.

 Game Boy Camera— This nifty add-on allows the user to take snapshots with the Game Boy, then edit the photos and include them in games or in self-created animations. It can also be used to create music or to mix two separate music tracks.

 Game Boy Printer—The Game Boy Printer allows users to print stickers directly from a Game Boy or Game Boy Color.

Game Boy Link Cable—Use this cable to connect the Game Boy to another Game Boy and play 2-player linked games.

Gameshark for Game Boy—This plug-in cartridge allows access to hidden characters, levels, and cheats for supported games. Nintendo does NOT support this product.

Sega Dreamcast

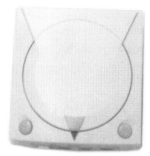

Prior to the release of the PlayStation 2, Sega's Dreamcast held the honor of having the most sophisticated graphics of any console system. Rendering over three million polygons per second, the Dreamcast hit the market with eye-popping visuals and quickly began eating up market share. However, as with the Nintendo 64, the Dreamcast has yet to approach the number of titles on the market that the PlayStation has. With fewer than 100 titles available as of this writing, the Dreamcast is still one of the new kids on the block.

The Dreamcast is Internet enabled, allowing you to hook up via the internal modem and surf the web, or battle it out with other players online. With 128-bit processing, 3D audio, the ability to play audio CDs, and a host of other features, the Dreamcast is a great game machine. It ships with the Dreamcast console (which includes four controller ports, a 56k modem port and a serial port), one standard Dreamcast controller, stereo A/V cable, phone cable, and Internet browser CD-ROM.

Dreamcast Technical Specifications

- 128-bit 3D processing power provides amazing lighting and other special effects
- Built-in 56kbps modem
- 24 megabytes of memory for huge, complex game worlds
- 64-voice CD-quality audio
- Four built-in controller ports for easy multiplayer action
- Built-in high-speed expansion ports

Control

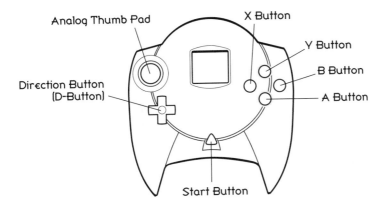

Analog Thumb Pad

X Button

Y Button

B Button

A Button

Direction Button
(D-Button)

Start Button

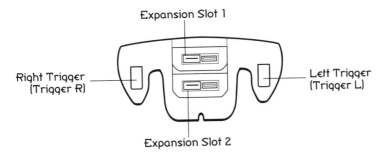

Expansion Slot 1

Right Trigger
(Trigger R)

Left Trigger
(Trigger L)

Expansion Slot 2

The Dreamcast controller is similar to that of the Nintendo 64, since it gives players the option of using either buttons or an analog stick to control the action. The expansion slot in each controller can be used to insert a Jump Pack or a VMU (Virtual Memory Unit)—Dreamcast's save-game unit that also doubles as a mini portable game machine in its own right.

Additional Products

In addition to the basic system that includes a controller and the Dreamcast console, you can also find the following accessories that enhance the Dreamcast experience.

Dreamcast Controller—With four controller ports and only one controller that ships with the console, you might consider purchasing one or more additional controllers, especially if your family has one or more additional players.

Jump Pack—Dreamcast's force-feedback expansion. The Jump Pack adds a whole new sensory experience to Dreamcast games, allowing the player to feel those explosions, collisions, and crashes.

Virtual Memory Unit—This ingenious device acts as a memory card, but also doubles as a game console a la the Game Boy. Supported games will feature mini-games that can be downloaded to the VMU. Players will also be able to download game characters for 'training,' or to transfer them to another Dreamcast system.

Concept 4 Racing Wheel— This is Dreamcast's steering wheel for driving games. It includes vibration feedback (like the Jump Pack) and a shift lever.

Fishing Controller—This is an interesting controller, to say the least. It's designed specifically for fishing games and features force-feedback to let the player know when he's hooked one (and when one has gotten away).

PC Platform: Windows and Macintosh

Computer games have been around about as long as computers. In many ways, the evolution of our current computer technology has been influenced by the cutting-edge technology necessary to play increasingly complex computer games. This section of the chapter is not about to cover all the intricacies of each computer type, nor is it going to assist you in evaluating either type of computer overall. Our focus here is on each platform as it relates to games, so keep that in mind as we continue.

Computers and Games

Personal Computers, Windows and Macintosh, were originally used primarily for business applications: things like spreadsheets, word processors, and computer-aided drafting. Early on in the history of home computers, however, industrious programmers soon realized that computers could also be used for a more entertaining pursuit: games.

The earliest computer games were called "text adventures." Without any form of graphical interface, these games contained massive amounts of written text that the user would read and react to, controlling their movement throughout the game world with now-archaic written commands. While these games now seem outmoded, many older computer users fondly remember them.

As computers became more powerful, it was only natural that these text adventures would begin to sport graphics. Early games like *Mystery House* and *Maniac Mansion* combined textual feedback with a graphical representation of the game world. While the graphics on games such as these were crude by today's standards, they paved the way for the completely graphical games of today.

The next major innovation in computer games was the rising prevalence of CD-ROM drives. Before computers were capable of reading Compact Discs, all software had to be sold on 3.5" floppy disks, which were only capable of holding 1.44 megabytes of data each. When CDs, each of which holds over 600 megabytes of data, became popular, game developers were able to use the extra space at their disposal to make larger games, with better graphics and residual innovations like digitized speech and full-motion video.

Chapter 2 • Game Platforms

Computer games have recently entered something of a renaissance, with two more new technology revolutions occurring at the same time. The rise of the Internet and the advances made in the field of three-dimensional graphics have both raised the standards of gamers, with game developers now competing to present both cutting-edge graphics and new and innovative uses of the Internet in their products. Perhaps as a side effect to the growth of the Internet, more people are playing computer games now than ever before.

With new technologies debuting every month, it's uncertain what the next major innovation will be for the computer game industry. Photo-realistic graphics and massively multiplayer online gaming will both be the standards within a few years, but where games go from there is anyone's guess. With the distinctions between computer and console slowly breaking down, it's entirely possible that gamers in the coming years will be migrating to high-tech consoles like the PlayStation 2 and X-Box, which are much cheaper than a high-powered PC, but at the cost of less versatility.

Without question, the two dominant personal computers are Windows-based machines—including Windows 3.1, 95, 98, 2000, Windows NT, and Windows ME—and Macintosh machines. Although Macintosh had the early edge in computer gaming, Windows has far surpassed it as the dominant player in the market.

Windows or Macintosh?

Microsoft's Windows operating environment, in all its incarnations, has become the most common computer game platform. Windows runs on compatible personal computers with varying system configurations, and although it is the most common, it's far from the simplest environment for new users. Macintosh, on the other hand, has always been the more user-friendly computer, making it far easier to launch a game (and most programs). However, since Windows dominates the PC market, developers and vendors (video card makers, CPU manufacturers, etc.) put much more emphasis on the platform.

The bottom line: If you want to be able to play the most games on a computer, then your choice should be a Windows-compatible machine.

Chapter 2 • Game Platforms

Microsoft Windows

In versions of Windows before Windows 95, users frequently had to run games in an archaic DOS mode to get them to work. In newer versions of Windows, the operating system is able to handle even the most processor and memory-intensive games from within the system.

The flexibility of the Microsoft Windows operating system lends itself well to support for computer games. Most users will admit to a love-hate relationship with Windows, given the amount of tinkering needed to setup everything just the way they like it. But with Direct X, Direct3D, and a host of other game-specific components, Windows has much to offer game developers, and by association, game players.

DirectX – What does it do?

By simplifying the process of developing three-dimensional graphics, sound effects, hardware support, and other multimedia features, the newest version of DirectX (7.0a as of this writing) allows computer game developers to concentrate on what they do best—making high-quality software. In essence, DirectX makes development for computers more like development for consoles, where the hardware is always the same. Given that much of a developer's time is spent working out compatibility problems across multiple hardware configurations, DirectX is a welcome tool to reduce the time spent on these issues.

Development of computer games is much more difficult than it is for console games. There are literally millions of possibilities when it comes to computer hardware, so it's impossible for game developers to create a game that covers every possible hardware-related issue. This is the biggest drawback to computer games under Windows—there's no guarantee that a given system will run a particular game.

When choosing a computer game, it's important that you carefully check the System Requirements found on the software packaging, and compare them to your system before your purchase. Failure to do this simple check can result in serious frustration, especially when it comes to graphics performance.

Computer graphics have received a tremendous amount of focus in recent years. With the advent of advanced 3D rendering using various 3D accelerated graphics cards (3dFx Voodoo, Nvidia, Riva, GeForce, and others), developers can create games that more closely resemble reality. With more raw power at their disposal, games can make full use of a computer system's components, and in many cases, adjust themselves to a particular hardware configuration.

Technical Specifications

There are as many possible system configurations for Windows PCs as there are users. It would be impossible for us to cover all of them, or even a representative sample. What we have provided below are the portions of your system likely to be highlighted on any game's packaging, along with a brief explanation of what each means. This is by no means an all-inclusive list, but it should give you an idea of what to expect.

Look for system requirements on the software packaging. They are usually on the bottom, side, or back of the box near the bar code.

Required Specifications

- **Processor speed**—You'll generally see an Intel Pentium-class processor speed requirement here, such as Pentium 233 Processor or Equivalent. Pay special attention to this requirement, and make sure your system complies before buying the game. There are few things more frustrating than trying to play a game on a system with a processor that can't handle it.
- **Operating System**—Usually Windows 95, 98, 2000, or NT
- **RAM requirement**—Simply put, RAM (Random Access Memory) is the where the game software stores instructions to the processor. Be sure that your system has enough RAM to meet the game's minimum requirement to insure optimum performance.
- **Hard Drive Space**—The minimum amount of hard drive space required to install the game.
- **DirectX requirement**—More often than not, new games will require DirectX in some form or other. Don't worry if you don't have it, or aren't sure if you do; most games will install the current version for you. DirectX is also available for free from the Microsoft website.
- **CD ROM speed**—You'll usually find a requirement for a minimum CD ROM speed, even if the CD ROM is only used during installation.
- **Video Card**—If the title is 3D accelerated, then you'll see a set of requirements for a separate 3D graphics card. If you don't have a 3D card, then you won't be able to run a title with this requirement.
- **Sound Card**—Any special requirements for your system's sound card will be listed here.

Recommended Specifications

Recommended specifications are different from required specifications. Most developers have created the game to be played optimally on a certain system configuration. This is the configuration they feel is most likely to give you the gaming experience they intend. They will then back off this optimal configuration, and come up with the "Required Specifications." Even though your system may meet the required specs for a particular game, you'll be much happier the closer your system mirrors the developer's recommendations.

Multiplayer Support

Any special requirements to play a game head-to-head, whether over the Internet or on a single PC, will be listed here.

Control

Most computer games are controlled with a combination of keyboard and mouse. It's also possible to attach a joystick or other peripheral controller. The only thing to take note of here is that it's important to make sure that there's not a requirement for a controller you don't have. A flight simulator that doesn't require a joystick is a rare thing; be sure you have the controller you need before buying a title.

Peripherals

A peripheral is any hardware component that can be attached to a computer system externally. Joysticks, steering wheels, external storage media (Zip, Jaz), and external video cameras are all examples of peripherals.

Macintosh

Way back in the old days (the 1970s), Apple launched their line of personal computers. As the first Windows PC was years away, the Apple systems enjoyed the focus of game developers. Over time, the Apple product line evolved into the Macintosh line we know today.

The Macintosh (or "Mac") platform is an excellent one, particularly because it avoids many of the system configuration nightmares that Windows users face on a daily basis. Hardware plugged into a Mac just works, with little or no need to tinker with systems setting as you sometimes do under Windows. In addition, the Macintosh platform is highly prized by graphics-intensive users. Many of the best design and art programs are created for this platform, rather than the Windows environment.

While there are plenty of game titles available for the Mac, it suffers because Windows is such a dominant force in the industry. Most titles are developed for the Windows environment first, then—if and only if they are highly successful—they are adapted for the Mac. In some cases, development for both environments is simultaneous, but this is extremely rare. For this reason, Macs lag far behind Windows PCs in the number of titles available. However, don't be discouraged—if you have a Mac, there are plenty of games available to keep you and your children happy.

Technical Specifications

Macintosh system specifications are much more streamlined than those of their Windows counterparts. Since each new generation of Mac is defined by its OS (Operating System), you'll see a requirement for a particular OS on any Mac software you purchase. For instance, the latest iteration is the Mac X ("Mac ten") OS. Any game that requires it as a base will have OS X or better on the packaging.

The Mac OS simplifies things immensely, since the assumption is that if your Mac is running the right OS, everything you need will be available, and the game will run as expected. You'll also see some of the following requirements on a Mac game box:

Required Specifications

- **Processor speed**—Check to make sure you have a fast enough system to run the game (i.e. Power PC 233MHz or faster).
- **RAM requirement**—As with Windows machines, Macs must have enough RAM to run a given title. Be sure your Mac meets this requirement for optimum performance.
- **Hard Drive Space**—The minimum amount of hard drive space you must have in order to install and run the game.
- **CD ROM requirement**—Indicates any CD ROM speed requirement for the game.

Recommended Specifications

As with Windows PCs, developers will provide what they feel is the optimal system configuration for a particular game. While you only need to have a system that meets the required specs, the closer your system is to the recommended specs, the better the games performance will be.

Multiplayer Support

Any special requirements for Multiplayer play will be outlined in this section of the System Specifications.

Control

Macs also use a combination of the keyboard and mouse for game control, but you can also attach peripherals such as a joystick or racing wheel for additional control. Requirements for any of these will appear on the game's packaging.

Future Platforms

At the time of this writing, there are several new game platforms in development that are well worth discussing, since they will be on the shelves by 2001, and directly competing with those already mentioned earlier. Information about some of these systems is sketchy at this point, but all boast more powerful capabilities than their predecessors and give gamers more options—never a bad thing.

Microsoft X Box

Kept tightly under wraps until March 2000, Microsoft is currently developing a proprietary game system dubbed the X Box. X Box is expected to offer advanced graphics, flexible Internet gaming, and realistic gameplay. Aimed squarely at the PlayStation 2, the X Box certainly has a significant power advantage and the support of an industry leader. (Not to mention their money; Microsoft is reportedly ready to spend over $500 million to market the system.) However, it remains to be seen if Sony's lead can be shaken, due to the large number of titles on the market for the PlayStation systems.

X Box System Specs

- 733 MHz IntelCPU
- 300 MHz custom-designed X-Chip graphics processor
- 64MB memory
- 4x DVD
- 8 GB Hard Disk
- 8 MB Memory card
- Broadband enabled
- DVD Movie playback

Chapter 2 • Game Platforms

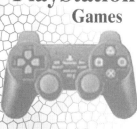

Nintendo's GameCube

Nintendo is hard at work on their next generation console system, dubbed the GameCube. Unlike the PlayStation 2, Nintendo has created a console that is more dedicated to games than future technology or being an entertainment "hub" for your home. Although it does have a DVD ROM and all the bells and whistles you'd expect from a newer console, the features of the GameCube are aimed primarily at the game market. Nintendo wants you to turn on the GameCube and play games—period.

In a true stroke of genius, the GameCube also has an interface for the handheld Game Boy Advance. The two connect via the game port, allowing the Game Boy Advance to control the action on the GameCube.

GameCube System Specs

- 0.18 Micron 405 MHz IBM copper chip CPU - "Gekko"
- 202.5mhz graphics provessor
- Image Processing Function: Fog, subpixel anti-aliasing, HW light x6, alpha blending, virtual texture design, multi-texture mapping, bump mapping, environment mapping, bilinear filtering, real-time texture decompression.
- Special 16bit DSP sound processing.
- Matsushita DVD drive capable of holding 4.3 GB of data.

Nintendo's Game Boy Advance

Besides busily developing their next generation console, Nintendo has their next generation hand-held Game Boy in the works. The Game Boy Advance will surpass the current Game Boy Color significantly, moving from the Game Boy Color's 8-bit processor to a new 32-bit processor. Nintendo also claims the mighty Game Boy Advance will support all old Game Boy Color games and have internet access for multiplayer games. Even with all of these improvements, Nintendo also reports that the Game Boy Advance will have double the battery life of the Game Boy Color! The preliminary systems specs seem to indicate that the Game Boy Advance will surpass the old Super Nintendo in capabilities, possibly leading to ports of old SNES titles. Rough estimates put the Game Boy Advance release sometime in the late 2000 or early 2001 timeframe.

One additional feature mentioned in our GameCube overview is that the Game Boy Advance can interface with the GameCube.

Game Boy Advance Preliminary System Specs

- 511 simultaneous colors in character mode, 32,768 in bitmap mode
- 65,535 colors available for new Game Boy Advance games
- 32-bit ARM processor with embedded memory
- 2.9" reflective screen running at 240x160 resolution
- 20 hours of game life on 2 AA batteries

Linux

A departure from our console-heavy list of future platforms is the computer operating system Linux. Hot on the heels of Microsoft, the grass roots Linux movement is catching fire. Linux is a user-friendlier version of the UNIX mainframe computer operating system, and it is enjoying increasing success in putting a dent in Microsoft Windows' market share.

Although Linux is still a dark horse at best, game developers have embraced the operating system. Most notably, id Software, one of the most influential game developers in the industry, has made a commitment to release Linux versions of their games along with Windows and Macintosh versions. Other developers are following suit, resulting in a groundswell of games experimenting with the OS.

It will be interesting to see how (and if) Linux can scratch its way into the market. There's no doubt that the recent Microsoft split can do nothing but help Linux, but only time will tell if the fledgling OS can overcome decentralized development and have a real impact on the market.

Platform Comparison

OK…we've discussed the various platforms, but if you're trying to decide which platform will suit your needs best, you're probably fairly confused. We've put together the table below to give you comparisons of the platforms. We've left out the Windows and Macintosh platforms, since your selection there is likely to revolve around your other PC needs more than on a comparison between them as game platforms. Also, we have not included the future platforms in the table below.

You may find that more than one platform will fit your needs, or you still may not be sure which to purchase. In either case, visit your retailer and try out the systems before you buy—most large chains (Babbages/Software Etc., CompUSA, etc.) have systems set up and running demo games in every store. Do your homework, and you'll be happier in the long run.

The tables below use a ranking system. In each category, the systems are rated from 1 (Best), to 5 (Worst), with 3 being Average. Each person is different, so you will most likely choose one or more categories that are important to you:

PlayStation
Games

- **Graphics**—This category ranks the systems by graphics performance.
- **# of Games**—This ranking awards top rating to the platform with the most titles on the market.
- **Portability**—A ranking of the ability to take the platform with you. If the platform requires the use of car adapters, it's ranked low, since this also requires the use of a portable television.
- **Multi-function**—Does the platform perform other functions besides game playing, such as Audio CD or DVD playing?
- **Internet**—Does the platform have Internet capabilities?

A lower overall score in the table above means that the platform met more criteria across the board than its competitors. However, as stated earlier, don't

Consoles

Category	PlayStation	PlayStation 2	Nintendo 64	Game Boy Color	Dreamcast
Graphics	4	1	3	5	2
# of Games	2	1*	4	3	5
Portability	5	5	5	1	5
Multi-function	2	1	2	3	2
Internet	5	1	5	5	2
Overall	18	9	19	17	16

* Includes the entire catalog of PlayStation games as well as its own.

judge by this lone criterion. For instance, if portability is important to you, and graphics aren't all that important, then you should select a Game Boy Color even though its overall ranking was third.

The table does highlight something that's reflected in the market—both the Nintendo 64 and Dreamcast are seriously threatened by the introduction of the PlayStation 2. The PlayStation is as well, but since most of its titles will work on the PS2, Sony wins either way. Expect to see fast-track development from Nintendo on their next generation system in order to keep up. As far as Sega's Dreamcast is concerned, Sega will need to capture as much market share as they can before the PlayStation2 and the rest of the next generation consoles hit the shelves. The end of 2000 and the beginning of 2001 will be a critical period for the platform

Chapter 3

Game Types and Genres

If you're new to some of the terms used in games today, it's probably a good idea for you to browse this chapter before diving into the rest of this guide. Here you'll find some definitions of the types of games on the market today, as well as the various genres on the shelves. This chapter doesn't include ratings, or specific game information; what you'll find here are some general terms used throughout the rest of this guide.

Most game developers create new titles with qualities similar to previous games. As in all industries, this is driven by sales—it's very rare for a company to create a game that has no basis on past successes. This establishes prominent gaming trends that fluctuate and evolve, much like fashion trends. Whenever a game with a new style of play becomes popular, it has the possibility of establishing a new gaming genre.

This chapter is designed to explain the current trends of gaming found on the PlayStation and PlayStation 2 systems. While this section does contain references to several games as examples, it is designed to give you a broad overview of what types of games are available for the PlayStation and PlayStation 2, rather than to provide an in-depth look at specific games.

Game Types

Single Player
Multiplayer

Genres

Action
   First Person
   Third Person
   Platform
   Tactical
   Fighting games
Adventure
Role Playing
Strategy
   Real-Time Strategy (RTS)
   Turn-Based Strategy
   Simulation
Sports
   Professional Sports
   Driving
   Recreational Sports
Puzzle
   Trivia
   Card & Board Games
   Pinball

Before We Begin...

Genre

Definition: A category of artistic composition, as in music or literature, marked by a distinctive style, form, or content—Webster's Revised Unabridged Dictionary

Before we jump into the game types and genres, it's worth pointing out a few things that might not be immediately obvious. First, there is no set list of genres that the industry has settled upon as a standard. Various publishers, developers, and even the press (both online and print media) tend to use similar descriptions to define genres. However, this isn't always the case. Don't assume that just because a game calls itself an action/adventure game that it has all the elements you'd expect from both genres—over time, the definitions of each genre have become watered down a bit.

This leads to the more important point—we are currently seeing a trend of genres blending together. In the old days (2-5 years ago), a game could be easily categorized in a particular genre. This is no longer the case, as an increasing number of games incorporate elements from several genres. It's very common to find games that are a melting pot of playing styles. In this section, we have given you examples of the basic genres, but we have not attempted to cover all the various combinations that are on the market today. It's safe to say that once you've read this chapter, you'll have enough information to get started, but there's no doubt that you should thoroughly check out a title through rental or other means before assuming that it's what you want.

Chapter 3 • Game Types and Genres

Game Types

Too many times, you pick up something in a store, read the package, and realize that you need an interpreter just to understand what's inside. If you've purchased a computer or console game lately, chances are you've experienced this. In an industry where new words and acronyms are invented every day, it's tough for insiders to keep up, let alone consumers. In this section, we'll cover a few of the more common types of games. These game types are actually a subset of the various game genres discussed later in this chapter.

There are two broad types into which most PlayStation and PlayStation 2 games fall. Many games released are specifically targeted toward either allowing only a single player to control game events or allowing multiple players to control game events. Technology permits many games today to support both types of play, but there are still many games that rely heavily on one aspect of the game, rather than both equally. The two types are explained in detail below.

Single Player

As the name implies, a single player game allows one player to control the action. In some cases, this indicates that only one player can play the game, but it can also mean that there is simply a single player element to a more diverse game. The bulk of PlayStation titles are primarily intended for a solitary player, but many also have multiplayer support of some fashion built-in. The same is generally true of PlayStation 2 titles, for now, but many titles do offer support for additional players. With an optional modem, and high-speed Internet support coming in the future, online games will no doubt be arriving for this system as soon as the hardware arrives to support them.

Single player games tend to have more involved storylines, so you will find that many adventure, role-playing, and strategy games are heavily single player focused. However, you can also find very good single player elements in action and sports games.

Multiplayer Games

Competition can bring out the best (and worst) in all of us. Unlike single player games, multiplayer games are designed to pit players against one another. Single player mode may be a game's primary focus, but it has become increasingly clear that games with a multiplayer component appeal to a fast-growing market.

For the PlayStation, multiplayer gaming involves two players sitting at the same console, using the two controller inputs to play a game simultaneously. Two more players can be added to the console through the use of an available expansion module. This form of multiplayer gaming, while rudimentary compared to the options available on the PC, can be quite fun. Most PlayStation games with multiplayer support will generally employ a "split-screen" view to allow the players to occupy different portions of the game world at the same time. Some, mostly sports and fighting games, are able to fit both players on the screen at the same time, eliminating the need for a split-screen view.

The situation is much the same with the PlayStation 2. Retaining the two controller ports of the original system, the same types of multiplayer options are available for this advanced system. In addition, the PlayStation 2 has an optional modem peripheral, allowing some games to be played over the Internet. In the coming years, Sony plans to roll out high-speed Internet access for the PlayStation 2. These options will allow players to interact with other players from all over the globe.

It's important to note that the best selling PC title of 1999, *Who Wants to be a Millionaire?*, is built around multiple players sitting at the same PC or console playing the game together. Nearly all multiplayer games allow you to play head-to-head on one computer, network, or console, but the fastest growing segment of multiplayer gaming is online games.

Chapter 3 • Game Types and Genres

Genres

Because the PlayStation 2 has not been released in the U.S. as of this writing, the games mentioned in this section of the guide include few PlayStation 2 titles. However, the PlayStation titles mentioned here are still representative of their genres, which is the point of this chapter. For a complete list of PlayStation 2 titles, please see Chapter 5: Game Reviews.

A game genre is simply a category that helps describe the basic content of a particular game. Much as the terms action, adventure, drama, and others can be used to categorize movies, the same holds true for video and computer games. Following are the most common genres used in the game industry. Many games fit into one or more categories—in fact, combining genres has become increasingly popular. Keep this in mind, because in many cases, these genres are used more as descriptions of game content than as hard and fast classifications.

Most modern games borrow concepts from different genres in an attempt to establish a unique style of gameplay. The groups listed below are often the most easily recognized genres but are by no means inflexible or fixed categories. Different game developers use different name classifications for their games, but the names used below are the most easily recognized genres in the industry.

Action

The action genre covers a broad range of games. At the most basic level, they all have one thing in common—they all require the player to be an active participant (or take some action) in nearly every part of the game in order to drive the story forward. In general, action games tend to be less reliant on intricate plots and in-game dialogue, and more dependent upon the player's interaction with the game.

Action games have classically been the most popular genre of games since the birth of electronic gaming. The fast-paced, adrenaline-inducing nature of action games has insured their popularity in modern electronic gaming market. Typically, action games require fast thinking and quick reflexes to win. It may only take one missed jump or one mistimed action to get your character killed or your vehicle destroyed. While action games have grown tremendously in complexity, the basic concepts have remained the same in today's PlayStation and PlayStation 2 games.

The action genre typically contains more violent games than other genres, but there is a very wide range in their violence level. Some action games contain no more violence than what can be seen on children's television shows, while others show violence that would be found only in PG-13 or R rated movies. As a parent, you should be aware that most of the games that have raised concerns about children and violence are action games. This doesn't mean that they are all bad. It does mean that you should more closely examine action titles to be sure they are what you want your children exposed to.

There are many games that fall into the action category, or that include some elements from this genre, and combinations of these various types are common. A few of the most common sub-genres within the action games genre are:

First Person

When the player's view of the game world is from a first-person perspective, the game is called a first person game. Usually, the only part of the player's virtual anatomy you can see in this type of game is a hand or a weapon being carried near the lower portion of the screen. Most of the first person games that appear on the PlayStation and PlayStation 2 are ports of popular PC games, such as *Quake 2*, though some titles, such as *Timesplitters* for the PlayStation 2, are original.

First person games generally pit the player against hordes of enemies, much like an action movie. The player controls his character, moving him or her through the game world, attempting to kill or evade enemies, collect weapons, and complete whatever objectives are necessary to proceed to the next level of the game. In general, these games are among the more violent titles on any platform, though some designers have attempted to soften the tone of their titles, either by substituting aliens, monsters, or other iconic foes for human enemies, or by replacing realistic guns with weapons like paintball guns and Nerf™ foam dart guns. Though some titles come with complex storylines, the dominant design for first person games is still one consisting mostly of visceral action. The increasing realism of the imagery in these games, especially in PlayStation 2 titles, may be too intense for younger players. However, there are only a handful of these titles available for either platform.

Ground Breaking Title: Quake II

This port of the popular PC game features various cyborg enemies and an array of futuristic weaponry. Players are cast in the role of a futuristic space Marine stranded during an invasion of an enemy planet, Stroggos. The goal is to destroy the Strogg and make it home alive. Players collect keys, explore the planet, and blow away everything in sight by using blasters, shotguns, machine guns, and more futuristic weapons. Rated "M" by the ESRB, this title is too violent for younger players, given the high level of animated blood and gore.

PlayStation First Person Games

Iron Soldier 3

Placing the player inside a giant 42-foot-tall robot, *Iron Soldier 3* requires players to complete a series of missions set in and around various cities. Players control the robot, or "mech" as it's commonly called, which has a huge arsenal at its disposal. With nearly everything in the game serving as cannon fodder—buildings, tanks, aircraft—players can rampage through the missions destroying everything in their path. In addition to the single player missions, *Iron Soldier 3* features split-screen multiplayer, allowing two players to go head-to-head on one system. *Iron Soldier 3* is rated "T" or Teen by the ESRB and includes animated violence.

PlayStation 2 First Person Games

Timesplitters

One of the first games available for the PlayStation 2, *Timesplitters* was designed by the same company that made the popular *007 Goldeneye* for the Nintendo 64. Players travel back and forth through various time periods, from 1935 to 2035, with the enemies and settings changing from each era. Along with an engaging single person game, *Timesplitters* also features an extensive multiplayer mode that includes several different types of play. As of this writing, this game is currently not rated by the ESRB.

Chapter 3 • Game Types and Genres

Third Person

A third person game includes a view of the entire character the player is controlling on-screen. Usually, the perspective is behind the character, allowing the player to easily control the character's actions.

These games are similar to first person titles, but the viewpoint allows for more exploration and acrobatics than is permitted by the real-world viewpoint of first person games. Since there is a higher degree of emphasis on the character design in third person games than in first person titles, there is generally a corresponding emphasis on a decent plot to thread the various levels together. Like the first person genre, the themes and content of third person games vary widely, so while one may be perfectly appropriate for all ages, another may be quite graphic.

There are many more third person games on the PlayStation than there are first person games, mostly due to the increased control these games give the player over the character.

Ground Breaking Title: Metal Gear Solid

Metal Gear Solid broke new ground on the PlayStation when it was released in 1997, requiring players to use stealth and cunning, rather than brute force alone to evade enemies and complete a series of missions. Players are cast in the role of Solid Snake, a retired super-spy who must infiltrate a terrorist base and defuse their plot. The game is unique because the characters in the game--mostly terrorist soldiers--will shoot Snake on sight, making it imperative that players use stealth and intelligence to complete the game. *Metal Gear Solid* is rated "M" by the ESRB and contains animated blood and violence.

PlayStation Third Person Games

Tomb Raider: The Last Revelation

The latest in the long-lived series of Tomb Raider games, *Tomb Raider: The Last Revelation* stars heroine Lara Croft as something of a female Indiana Jones. The emphasis here is on action, and players navigate Lara through increasingly difficult areas. The series is known for its puzzles, and this fourth installment has plenty of them. This game is rated "T" or Teen by the ESRB and contains animated blood and violence.

Tenchu 2: Birth of the Stealth Assassins

One of the rare games that can claim to be better than its predecessor, *Tenchu 2* puts the player in the virtual shoes of Rikamaru and Ayame, two ninjas in feudal Japan. The gameplay requires a high degree of stealth, but there is still plenty of action as well. Players are encouraged to flatten themselves against walls and stay quiet in order to avoid detection. The game itself is quite large, with 29 missions total. As you would expect from this game's title, it is rated "M" by the ESRB for including animated blood, gore, and violence.

PlayStation 2 Third Person Games

Oddworld: Munch's Oddysee

This game is actually the third installment in the Oddworld series, but it's one of the first titles released for the PlayStation 2. *Oddworld: Munch's Oddysee* is truly a game that must be seen and played to experience. Players are cast in the role of either of two unlikely heroes—Munch or Abe, the hero of the two earlier releases in this series—and will use whichever one of them is appropriate to complete various portions of their quest. The style of this game is unique, making it a must to check out at rental, and a solid addition to any PlayStation 2 collection. As with most PlayStation 2 titles, this game is currently not rated by the ESRB.

Gunslinger

In *Gunslinger*, the player is a gun-toting cowboy who has been wronged by an evil land baron. While the story isn't exactly original, it is unique to console games. This game is unique because of its third person perspective, and also because it allows the player to choose whether the character becomes a hero or a vile, wanted outlaw. This title is currently not rated by the ESRB.

Platform or Side-Scroller

The platform genre takes its name from some of the most popular games on the old Nintendo Entertainment System, such as *Mario Brothers, Donkey Kong*, and *Contra*. Most let the player control a character from a "side-scrolling" viewpoint, and the main character moves from left to right jumping from platform to platform as the background scrolls across the screen.

However, the platform genre has come to encompass a number of different styles of games, from the high-speed antics of *Sonic the Hedgehog* in the Sonic Adventure titles for the Dreamcast, to the relatively slow-paced play of *Rayman 2*, which has been ported to a number of platforms. The emphasis, however, is still on iconic characters and cartoonish action. The pace of platform games is generally quite fast, forcing players to rely more on sheer reflexes and quick wits than any kind of strategic planning. The animated, vibrant characters often make these games good choices for younger players, while the speed and graphics of the newer titles will attract older players.

The most famous example of these types of games on the PlayStation is the *Crash Bandicoot* series, currently spanning three platform games and a cartoonish racing game, with a multiplayer-oriented puzzle and party-game title coming soon. Due to the easily recognizable characters in platform games, they often become a kind of spokesperson for their respective system. *Crash Bandicoot* fills that role for the PlayStation, just as Mario fills it for the Nintendo systems.

> ### Ground Breaking Title: Crash Bandicoot
>
> *Crash Bandicoot* was Sony's attempt to create a mascot for their platform, similar to *Mario* for Nintendo and Sega's *Sonic the Hedgehog*. The original in this series has Crash navigating a jungle environment, spinning into enemies and smashing crates filled with fruit. The perspective is from behind our hero Crash, and the world is rendered in pseudo-3D, even though some portions of the game are throwbacks to old side-scrolling games. *Crash Bandicoot* was given a Kids to Adult rating—the ESRB's old designation for an "E" or Everyone title.

PlayStation Platform Games

Gauntlet Legends

This continuation of the venerable *Gauntlet* game, originally an arcade hit, features a top-down view of the action. The player chooses to be a wizard, warrior, valkyrie—a female warrior—or an archer, and then proceeds through the levels, attempting to stay alive and find secret areas and items. The game is large, and features support for multiple players. This title is rated "T" for Teen by the ESRB, and contains animated blood and violence.

Gex 3: Deep Cover Gecko

Like many other platform games, the Gex series uses an animal as its protagonist; in this case, it's Gex the Gecko attempting to rescue his fellow secret agent, Agent Xtra. He performs this task by exploring various locales, attempting to find enough remote controls to proceed to the next television-themed level. The 3D world is nice for the PlayStation, but the sexual innuendo given by Agent Xtra may be too risqué for younger children. It's interesting to note that although this title is rated "E", or suitable for Everyone, on the Nintendo 64, it is rated "T" for Teen for containing suggestive themes on the PlayStation and PC.

Tactical

This relatively new type of action game stresses the goal of completing missions and establishing teamwork more than glorifying the individual player him (or her) self. Most of these games are military in nature, requiring players to take a team through the entire game without losing them, generally from a first person or third person perspective. A common element of these games is a greater requirement for problem solving, as well as the need to use stealth to reach an objective.

As of this writing there are no Tactical titles slated for release on the PlayStation 2.

> **Ground Breaking Title: Spec Ops**
>
> In *Spec Ops*, the player is a member of the U.S. Special Operations Ranger Corps. The mission varies from level to level, but the player generally has to defend a position or attack an enemy fortification, in order to rescue hostages, for example. The game is quite difficult, with incredibly shrewd enemies, as well as grenades, booby traps, and mines to deal with. The player can issue commands to an AI-controlled teammate, which provides at least some small help. As you would expect, this game is rated "T" or Teen for including animated blood and violence.

Chapter 3 • Game Types and Genres

PlayStation Tactical Games

Rainbow Six

Based on the best-selling Tom Clancy novel of the same name, as well as being a port of the highly successful PC game, *Rainbow Six* allows the player to control a squadron of anti-terrorist troops. Most often, the missions require the player to infiltrate a structure where hostages are being held, and either kill or incapacitate the terrorists, while safeguarding the hostages.

Fighting games

The fighting genre came into its own with the release of classic games like *Street Fighter 2* on the Super Nintendo, and has been a mainstay of console gaming ever since. They generally have one goal: beat the virtual opponents that stand between you and victory. There are many different styles of fighting games, including boxing, wrestling, martial arts, street fighting, and more. All of them require players to focus on learning special hit combinations and moves to advance through the enemies and win the game. Good eye-hand coordination is a must for any fighting game.

Like any other genre, the content of fighting games varies widely from title to title. Some are relatively mundane and cartoonish, like the popular *Ready 2 Rumble Boxing*. Many, however, are quite realistic in their depictions of violence, complete with breaking bones and animated blood. To make things more complicated, most PlayStation titles offer somewhat cartoonish creatures mixed in with humans, pummeling each other into submission with a variety of throws and special moves. The popular *Tekken* series, for instance, is known for its multiple secret characters, which become available for play once unlocked by the player, whether through a secret code or some special achievement within the game itself. These characters range widely in form, from panda bears and lizards to even more bizarre creatures. Some games, like the *Bushido Blade* series, strive for a more realistic simulation of close-range combat.

> ## Ground Breaking Title: Mortal Kombat
> *Mortal Kombat* is an arcade classic that made the transition to console games very easily. Pitting two players against one another in a fight to the death, *Mortal Kombat* is easily one of the most violent game series around. The PlayStation versions of this classic (*Mortal Kombat Trilogy*, *Mortal Kombat 4*, and *Mortal Kombat Special Forces*) feature very realistic animation. Although the original game featured cartoon-like blood, recent versions feature photo-realistic violence, with blood spraying and other more gruesome animations. Needless to say, no *Mortal Kombat* title has ever received a rating lower than "T" or Teen on the ESRB rating scale, and many are rated "M" or Mature. This doesn't lessen the impact that this series has had on the genre. To many fighting game experts, *Mortal Kombat* is still the benchmark against which all other fighting titles are measured.

PlayStation Fighting Games

Marvel vs. Capcom

In *Marvel vs. Capcom*, the players control fighters taken from both Capcom's *Street Fighter* series, as well as characters from a number of Marvel Comics, such as the X-Men, Spider-Man, and Captain America. The gameplay is more cartoonish than most fighting games, with emphasis on creating huge combinations of blows (which can become quite impressive). This game is rated "T" or Teen by the ESRB for containing animated violence.

X-Men: Mutant Academy

This recent title plays very similarly to *Marvel vs. Capcom*, though it only features the X-Men characters. As in many fighting games, there is no blood here, even when Wolverine uses his claws on an opponent. Like the Capcom game, players attempt to beat their opponent until they can land a large combination of blows on him or her. This title is rated "T", or Teen, for containing animated violence.

PlayStation 2 Fighting Games

Tekken Tag Tournament

This game, the latest in the long-lived *Tekken* series, is one of the first fighting games available for the PlayStation 2. Sporting highly detailed characters and backgrounds, *Tekken Tag Tournament* allows players to control a vast array of different fighters, even switching between them in the middle of a fight, hence the "tag" in the title. The hand-to-hand combat is fairly brutal, with crunching bones and a variety of special moves designed to pummel the opponent. This title is currently not rated by the ESRB.

Dead or Alive 2

Dead or Alive 2 is a slick 3D fighting game that allows movement in and out of interactive environments during the course of a battle. More than most other fighting games, the environment will affect the fighting, making it as important to master the arenas as it is to master the moves used to win. This title has appeared on the Dreamcast system, and was rated "T" or Teen for animated violence and suggestive themes. It is currently not rated by the ESRB on the PlayStation 2.

Chapter 3 • Game Types and Genres

Adventure

Adventure games have been around since the early days of video games. These games are heavily geared toward plot development, and they typically require the player to choose certain actions, solve puzzles, and find information to advance the story. Many of these titles include cinematic or video sequences that help to move the plot along. Whether they are set in the distant future, present day, or some other fantasy world, adventure games are about exploration and discovery. The selection of adventure games for console systems is somewhat limited; most adventure games are created for the PC platform. However, an adventure title that sells well on the computer will eventually make it to a console in one form or another.

Perhaps the most successful adventure game series on the PlayStation are the *Resident Evil* games from Capcom. These unique titles attempt to place the character in something of a classic horror B-movie, complete with mysterious mansions, puzzles, and roving zombies. Dubbed "survival horror," the adventure genre that *Resident Evil* has spawned on the PlayStation include various sequels, as well as original games from other companies. As indicated by the name of the genre, the point of these games is generally just to survive against overwhelming odds. These games can sometimes be frustrating and difficult, and the content will likely be too graphic for younger players. A good rule of thumb is to treat these games as you would a horror film. If you wouldn't let a child watch a *Friday the 13th* movie, for instance, these probably wouldn't be a good choice either.

This doesn't mean that all adventure games on the PlayStation and PlayStation 2 are of this variety; some are more light-hearted affairs, so be sure to examine the game's ESRB rating and descriptions before disregarding it.

> ### Ground Breaking Title: Covert Ops: Nuclear Dawn
> This game puts the player in the shoes of Jack Morton, an Air Force Lieutenant who has been ordered to protect the French Ambassador while he travels on a military train, the Blue Harvest. After the train is hijacked by terrorists, Jack must fight his way through all 16 cars, attempting to rescue the Ambassador and his family. This game is rated "M" by the ESRB, and contains animated blood, gore, and violence.

PlayStation Adventure Games

Resident Evil

While the title of this survival-adventure game alone will offend some parents, this section wouldn't be complete without mentioning it. As one of the most influential titles on the PlayStation, *Resident Evil* puts the player in the role of a member of an elite team, who enter an old mansion after a previous team has been lost inside. Zombies are loose in the creepy house, and players will have to navigate various puzzles, and use their wits as much as brute force in order to get out alive. *Resident Evil* is rated "M" by the ESRB, and contains animated blood, gore, and violence.

Dino Crisis

From Capcom, the makers of the original *Resident Evil* games, comes *Dino Crisis*, which replaces the zombie opponents of the *Resident Evil* series with dinosaurs, but leaves most of the core gameplay in place. While the scares and violence might be too much for younger children, older players will enjoy the intricate plot. This game is rated "M" by the ESRB, and contains animated blood, gore, and violence.

Role Playing

Role playing games, or RPGs as they are commonly called, cover a broad range of titles. In the purest sense, RPGs are games in which the player creates a character that lives and breathes in the game, and as the game progresses, the character's attributes—skills acquired while playing the game—change with experience. A player may select the skills they wish to practice, allowing each player to influence the direction their character's life takes within the game.

On the PlayStation and PlayStation 2, most RPGs are games that are translated and localized for American audiences from the original Japanese (though, of course, there are some titles, like *Summoner* for the PlayStation 2, that were created in America). Many, if not all, follow a rather standard "epic" storyline: a small group of characters must fight against a large dictatorial organization to save the world, or something similar. The common Japanese influence results in what are often complex, involving (and often quite long) storylines, filled with a multitude of unique characters.

Heavy interaction with other characters is a must in RPG games, since the plot (and the character's attributes) is heavily dependent upon the encounters with the other characters. Many RPGs got their start as table-top or "pen and paper" games, such as *Dungeons & Dragons*, but not all RPGs are set in fantasy worlds. Any game that allows the player to create and mold a character throughout the game is said to have an RPG element, so many titles fit this mold in some way or other. If this is the primary focus of the game, however, then the game will be labeled a true RPG.

Computer RPGs and console RPGs are usually very different games. On computers, RPGs tend to be vast, sprawling worlds that players explore in real-time and near-realistic graphic detail. These RPGs more closely resemble the old table-top *Dungeons & Dragons* games. Console RPGs are usually more whimsical, depending upon deep character development and interaction with other characters across wide-ranging worlds—players may never see everything there is to see in the game due to the sheer size and scope of some of these titles.

Ground Breaking Title: Final Fantasy

Few games have reached the legendary status of Square's *Final Fantasy* series. The most recent release in the series, *Final Fantasy VIII*, is also one of the most lavish productions in video game history, reportedly costing over $30 million to make. In similar fashion to the other seven titles in the series, the player controls a party of adventurers, participating in bloodless battles against fantastic, though realistic, enemies. Scattered throughout the gameplay are some stunning cinematic scenes, featuring computer-generated imagery to rival any Hollywood movie. The typically deep and long plot, with a romance between two main characters at its heart, may go over the heads of younger players, but even those who might not grasp the intricacies of the storyline will enjoy the core gameplay. The games in the *Final Fantasy* series have consistently been rated "T" or Teen for including animated violence. More recent titles also include mild language and suggestive themes.

PlayStation Role Playing Games

Legend of Mana

Another RPG from Square, *Legend of Mana*, might not boast the production values of *Final Fantasy VIII*, though the graphics are a bit friendlier than the sometimes dark and moody world of the last Final Fantasy installments. The plot is less coherent, as well, consisting mainly of smaller quests rather than one large epic plot.

Alundra 2

Although the sequel has little to do with the first title in this two-game series, *Alundra 2* puts the player in the role of Flint, whose parents have been killed by pirates. Fleeing for his life, Flint runs into various characters in his travels, including, of course, the pirates, a princess, and an evil but quirky sorcerer. *Alundra 2* is rated "T" by the ESRB and contains mild animated violence.

PlayStation 2 Role Playing Games

Summoner

One of the first RPGs for the PlayStation 2 surprisingly comes from American developer Volition. This is surprising not only due to the fact that most RPGs are originally Japanese, but also because Volition is best known for their work on the *Freespace* series of space combat games for the PC. *Summoner* allows the player to control Joseph, a young man who has the power to summon demons. After he accidentally destroys his hometown, he is the target of an assassination attempt. After his bare survival, Joseph must find out who wants to kill him, aided by up to four other party members. This game is currently not rated by the ESRB.

Strategy

Strategy games require some form of strategic thinking in order for players to complete them. Most of the titles in this genre are military in nature—whether the setting is a historical battle, or conflict on some imaginary planet—but not all strategy games are based on military conflicts. The basic element of any strategy title begins with a set of resources (troops, equipment, resources) which the player must use wisely in order to defeat the enemy or other players in the game. Resource management is crucial to strategy games, as is the development of new technology through ongoing research. If the game is centered around a historical battle or situation, then the player won't be able to add resources as the game progresses. However, some of the most popular titles in this genre allow players to develop their resources and grow their forces (or their Empire) as the game progresses.

There are three subsets in this genre. Any of them can be combined to describe a strategy title. As with genres in general, these started out as separate categories, but over time, the lines between them have blurred. Newer strategy titles may incorporate any of these subsets.

Real-Time Strategy

A real-time strategy (or RTS) game requires that the player make all decisions while the clock is ticking. The game world (and thus the war) goes on around the players while they make their decisions. This challenging game type is tremendously popular on the PC, but very few RTS games are made for console systems, due to the unwieldy controllers, which inhibit the precise pointer control needed to succeed in these games.

> ### Ground Breaking Title:
> ### Command & Conquer - Red Alert
> Although a much better seller on the PC platform, *Command & Conquer - Red Alert*—sequel to the massive best-seller *Command & Conquer*—is a prime example of a real-time strategy game. Players begin missions with a basic set of military units, then are forced to complete objectives. Gameplay is a fine balance between adding resources (units) and completing the objectives within mission parameters. *Command & Conquer - Red Alert* is rated "T", or Teen, by the ESRB and contains realistic violence.

PlayStation Real-Time Strategy Games

Dune 2000

This game is based on the classic *Dune* novels by Frank Herbert. Players control one of three factions vying for control of the resources on the planet Dune. Like most RTS games, players build factories and harvest resources in order to construct an army of units to crush their opponents. This game is rated "T" or Teen by the ESRB and contains animated and realistic violence.

PlayStation 2 Real-Time Strategy Games

War Monkeys

Developed by Silicon Dreams, *War Monkeys* takes place in the year 2161 on a small planet called Primus IV. Three opposing forces wage war in a full 3D environment. The game features a powerful rendering engine, capable of displaying up to 200 individual units onscreen at once, and can mimic battlefields up to 25 kilometers in size. This game is not yet rated by the ESRB.

Turn-Based Strategy

A turn-based strategy (or TBS) game stops the clock while players make decisions on the battlefield. These games play more like traditional table-top games such as chess, where one player makes a move and then waits for the other player's move before moving again. Most of the TBS games for the PC are militaristic in nature, but the titles that have been made for the PlayStation have typically been more along the lines of console RPGs, with fantasy environments and magic-using characters, resulting in the "strategy RPG" moniker that is often applied to them. At this point, there are no true turn-based strategy games for the PlayStation 2.

> ### Ground Breaking Title: Final Fantasy Tactics
>
> This turn-based strategy game is based on the Final Fantasy series of games from Square. The depth of the plot isn't typical of most TBS games, being much more intricate than many of its PC counterparts, and there is plenty of gameplay to match, with some of the most impressive graphics seen in this genre on the PlayStation. The action is cartoonish, with many of the same spells and characters as the "real" Final Fantasy games.

Vandal Hearts 2

This game features a turn-based battle system with a plot that would seem typical of an RPG, with a small group of warriors struggling against steep odds. Players move their characters around a large world map, and engage in battles on a variety of battlefields. In a slight twist, the game's artificial intelligence is at work during your "turn," adding to the strategic elements of the game. This game is rated "M" by the ESRB, and contains animated blood, gore, and violence.

Simulation

Simulations are usually more heavily focused on building something than they are on combat or conflict. In most simulations, the goal is to create something, manage the world around it to cause it to flourish, and basically help it to evolve into some future state. Titles in this category can also include simulations of real-world activities such as flight simulations. The best-known example of this category is *Sim City*, now regarded as a classic for its innovative gameplay and in-depth simulation of a modern city. None of the many iterations of *Sim City* have made it to the PlayStation, but the PlayStation's drought of this type of title is about to end. While most of these games are intended for the PC, a few are ported to the PlayStation and PlayStation 2.

PlayStation Simulation Games

Ground Breaking Title: Populous: The Beginning

This PlayStation simulation game puts the player in the role of a deity, responsible for guiding a fledgling tribe through a variety of missions, while fending off worshipers of rival deities in an Iron-age world. As a deity, players have control over virtually every aspect of the world, and can either assist their followers or devastate rival factions at will by causing natural disasters. This game is rated "T" by the ESRB for containing animated violence.

PlayStation 2 Simulation Games

Theme Park World

One of the PlayStation 2's launch titles, *Theme Park World*, is a game that allows the player to build and maintain a virtual theme park. Along with building the actual park, players must manage nearly every aspect of the park, including regulating traffic flow and making sure that guests remain happy. This title is not yet rated by the ESRB.

Sports

Games that focus on real-world sports are very popular. This genre's name is self-explanatory; if it's a sport, then chances are that someone somewhere has created a console or PC version of it. There are three important sub-genres within sports games.

Professional Sports

In order to provide some separation, we've broken out any sport that is played by professional teams (football, baseball, soccer, hockey, etc.) into this group. There are two types of professional sports games: those with a license from the league they're attempting to recreate, and those without. A licensed game will feature real-world teams and players. Non-licensed games, which are becoming rare, might feature a star player's endorsement, but will have nameless or imaginary teams.

It's worth noting that nearly every professional sports game has been given an "E" rating by the ESRB, since there is no objectionable content in most of them.

Licensing

"Real-world" properties such as sports teams (and stars), movies, books, board games, and even popular toys such as Barbie have entered the electronic entertainment industry with a bang. Growth in officially licensed products as video or computer games is exponential, resulting in cross-pollination between traditional and electronic media. It's becoming increasingly likely that the distribution for any new form of entertainment--book, movie, game, or audio—or sports franchise, will include some form of computer or console game as an additional product placement in the market.

Ground Breaking Title: MLB 2001

One of the most recent baseball games for the PlayStation, the officially licensed *MLB 2001* includes all of the major-league baseball players and teams. In addition to the usual baseball simulation, *MLB 2001* also features a "manager mode" that allows the player to manage the team instead of playing through an entire season. This is a prime example of a professional sports game. As is common with this sort of game, the ESRB has given it a "E" for everyone.

Chapter 3 • Game Types and Genres

PlayStation Professional Sports Games

NBA Live 2000

Basketball, anyone? The sixth in the line of NBA Live games, the 2000 edition has all of the features that its predecessors enjoyed, with a few new ones to boot. All of the real NBA players are here, as well as some past All-Stars, such as Larry Bird and Magic Johnson, to provide variety.

PlayStation 2 Professional Sports Games

Madden NFL 2001

A launch title for the PlayStation 2, this is the first of what will likely be a long-running series for the platform, as the Madden NFL games appeared with yearly updates on the PlayStation. *NFL 2001* takes advantage of the power of the PlayStation 2, with excellent graphics, including a full NFL license and announcing by Pat Summerall and John Madden.

Ready 2 Rumble Round 2

Over-the-top pro wrestling at its finest is the premise of *Ready 2 Rumble Round 2*, one of the first releases for the PlayStation 2. Originally a Dreamcast game, this title comes to the PlayStation 2 with better graphics, more characters (all fan favorites plus many more) and even some special secret characters. This game is not yet rated by the ESRB.

Driving

The driving category of games rivals action for the sheer variety of games within it. Virtually any kind of fantastic or cartoonish scenario imaginable has been created within a driving game, along with the more serious driving simulations that are also popular. Therefore, there are two subsets of this sub-genre.

Simulation

Driving simulation games attempt to recreate the feel of real driving, whether in a race car, motorcycle, or other vehicle. Two of the more popular series have recently issued new games.

> ### Ground Breaking Title: Gran Turismo 2
>
> The first *Gran Turismo* was one of the deepest racing simulations ever made for the PlayStation, and the sequel has become even more popular than the original. Though there is an arcade mode that is interesting in its own right, the outstanding feature of the game is the simulation mode, where over 500 fully licensed cars are faithfully recreated from their real-world counterparts. There's a lot of gameplay here for racing fans. This game is rated "E" for everyone by the ESRB.

PlayStation Racing Simulations

NASCAR 2000

With 18 courses from the NASCAR circuit and 33 real-world drivers, this is one of the most extensive re-creations of the popular sport. Players can also create their own cars and race in a virtual NASCAR season, or choose among various mini-games for less time-consuming entertainment. This title is rated "E" by the ESRB and is suitable for everyone.

PlayStation 2 Racing Simulations

NASCAR 2001

Making a quantum leap graphically for the PlayStation 2 console, *NASCAR 2001* contains all the best features of *NASCAR 2000*, and adds several more. Cars show the actual damage inflicted during the race, giving drivers a good visual representation of exactly how beaten up their cars are. One of the most impressive things about this game is the realistic physics, which come into play during crashes as well as during smooth driving conditions. This title is not yet rated by the ESRB, but expect an "E" rating given the history of this series and the genre in general.

Arcade

Arcade racing games differ from other racing games in that they attempt to entertain the player with various fantastic locales and racing that is less constrained by the laws of physics. Crashes rarely end a race, as they would in a true simulation, with the players generally pressing a button to get back on the track, with a small time penalty. A few of these games even take combat into consideration, with cars that can shoot missiles or lay down oil slicks to hamper their opponents. The popularity of arcade racers has exploded on console platforms in the last few years.

Ground Breaking Title: Driver

One of the most unique driving games on any platform, *Driver* places the player in the shoes of an undercover police officer, who has to perform as a all-purpose driver for a Mafia family to earn their trust and eventually take them down. One of the most popular games on the system, this is one of the few games that was actually ported to the PC after debuting on a console. Cars can be damaged, though this takes more time than it would in real life. The main gameplay consists of the player attempting to complete objectives in a musclecar, while avoiding cops and keeping the car intact.

PlayStation Arcade Driving Games

Hydro Thunder

One of the few water-based racing games, *Hydro Thunder* places the player aboard a high-speed racing boat, racing against a number of computer-controlled players to be the first to the finish line. The player can collect various power-ups along the way, such as speed boosters or weapons, that will knock other players out of the way. This title is rated "E" by the ESRB.

Crash Team Racing

Crash Team Racing is based on the various characters from the Crash Bandicoot games, and is a more cartoonish, iconic racing game than most (similar to the *Mario Kart* series for the Nintendo systems). Younger players will enjoy the relatively simple racing effects that this game has to offer, and its "E" rating assures that it's fit for all ages.

PlayStation 2 Arcade Driving Games

World Destruction League: Thunder Tanks

World Destruction League: Thunder Tanks is the latest installment in a series called *Battle Tanx*. In a war-torn post-apocalyptic future, tank pilots battle it out for sport. As you would expect, drivers can blast opponents off the raceways, which include tracks in various environments. This title is not yet rated by the ESRB.

Recreational Sports

Hunting, fishing, and other recreational pastimes fit into this subset of sports games. Special controllers, such as virtual fishing reels, and even pistols have been developed to augment some of the more popular titles. The most popular variants, however, simulate the various sports that are popular with young people, such as skateboarding and stunt-biking. At this point, none of these titles are available for the PlayStation 2.

> **Ground Breaking Title: Action Bass**
> Released in mid-2000, *Action Bass* is a fast-paced arcade-style fishing game. Gameplay allows players to select a lure, then cast and land fish. The game is divided into several areas, and players are required to catch a certain number of fish in each area before time expires. This adds a speed element that requires careful lure selection to progress to the next area. This title is rated "E" by the ESRB.

Puzzle

Puzzle games cover a broad range of game titles. As you would expect, many of them require players to solve puzzles. Most puzzle games appear on computers. It's rare for these games to be ported to consoles, but it does occasionally happen if the title has been particularly successful on the computer. Puzzle games include unique and somewhat oddball games such as *Sheep, Lemmings,* and *Bust-a-Move.* However, there are other subsets within this genre.

Trivia/Game Show

Sports trivia games, world trivia games, general knowledge games, even ABC's popular television show *Who Wants to Be a Millionaire?* and the venerable *Jeopardy!* have all been re-created in either video game or PC game form. Not many games of this type are created for the more action-oriented PlayStation, and none are yet available for the PlayStation 2, though *You Don't Know Jack* is a notable exception.

> **Ground Breaking Title: You Don't Know Jack**
> One of the few trivia games on the PlayStation, *You Don't Know Jack* is a mock game show, with questions that are intended to be more humorous than challenging (though they can be quite obscure). Soon to be followed with a sequel, this game is fun to play in groups of 4 or more people. *You Don't Know Jack* is rated "T" or Teen for containing comic mischief, strong language, and suggestive themes.

Card & Board Games

Any board game can be included in this subset, including classics such as chess and mahjong. *Risk, Monopoly, Poker, Blackjack*—these are some of the best-selling games on the shelves.

Scrabble

This adaptation of the classic word game comes complete with Merriam-Webster's Official Scrabble Player's Dictionary, and has support for four human players, with computer-controlled players taking any unfilled spots. Unlike the real *Scrabble*, there is unfortunately no fibbing or creative word creation possible—the game verifies each word for authenticity before issuing points.

Family Game Pack

The *Family Game Pack* from 3DO is a collection of board and casino games, such as *Blackjack, Solitaire, Hearts*, and *Dominoes*, with almost two dozen games and variations altogether. There's a good amount of game-play built-in, and it's a value title as well, though the interface and graphics may disappoint players used to 3D flair from their PlayStation.

Pinball

While not actually puzzles, virtual pinball games are typically included in this genre. Again, not many games of this type are created for the PlayStation.

PlayStation Pinball Games

Pro-Pinball

Though somewhat hampered by the fact that there's only one table to play on, *Pro-Pinball* looks good and plays well, with elevated rails, multiple balls, magnets, ramps, and many other features found in modern pinball machines.

Chapter 4

What is the ESRB?

With all the concern about games and their influence on our children, wouldn't it be nice if a rating system existed that allowed parents to see at a glance if a game is appropriate for their child? Good news—there is an industry-accepted rating system already in place, and it's administered by an organization called the Entertainment Software Rating Board, or ESRB. Much as the motion picture industry's Motion Picture Association rates movies on a recognized scale, the ESRB performs the same important role in the electronic entertainment industry. However, it's still a little-known organization, and many parents are unaware of the services the ESRB provides. In this chapter, we'll cover:

> As this book went to press, two of the nation's largest retailers—Kmart and Wal-Mart—took steps to ensure that children could not purchase games rated 'M' (those intended for players over 17) by the ESRB in their stores. Both have installed scanning technology that prompts clerks to ask for ID if an M-Rated game is scanned at checkout. One thing is certain—with rising concern about M-Rated games getting into the hands of underage teens, more retailers may well follow the two giants' lead, possibly resulting in a reduced market for developers of M-Rated titles. With fewer retail outlets, many developers will make certain that their games are not rated M to insure placement in the maximum number of stores—much in the same way that movie studios carefully avoid the NC-17 movie rating for their product.

ESRB Background

Despite the massive growth in video and PC games during the 1980s and early 1990s, there was virtually no one looking at rating game content. After all, games' representation of reality during this period was fairly poor, so there seemed to be little need for the industry to self-regulate or to develop standards by which games were rated.

This slowly began to change as new technology allowed game developers to close the gap with reality. As we've approached the ability to graphically mirror reality, the content of games has also approached reality. Violence in games, including graphic depictions of death, dismemberment, and other gruesome scenes has greater impact now than ever before. Sexual themes can also be rendered in (for most parents) an uncomfortably realistic manner. Basically, if it can be viewed in a movie theater, it's now likely to be a possibility in video and computer games. Although it's every adult's choice to view or play whatever game they want, before 1994 there was no universally accepted body that rated game content so that consumers and parents would know whether a particular game was something they wanted to bring home.

Enter the ESRB. The Entertainment Software Rating Board (ESRB) is an independent rating system, which was established in September of 1994 by the Interactive Digital Software Association (IDSA), the leading trade association for the interactive entertainment software industry. The ESRB is a voluntary rating system which was developed to give parents and consumers information about the content of video and computer games so that they can make informed purchase and rental decisions. As of January 1998, the ESRB has rated over 5,000 titles submitted by over 300 publishers, making it by far the leading entertainment software rating system in the country and the only one which has rated software for all platforms, including personal computers, CD-ROMS and video game cartridge consoles.

It's impressive to note that while the motion picture industry took decades to develop an accepted ratings standard, the ESRB has developed one that is widely accepted within a very short time period (six years as of this writing). The speed of the system's development and acceptance is a testimony to the importance of this organization. Although the submission of a game to the ESRB is voluntary, the majority of retailers simply will not carry a non-educational game that doesn't have an ESRB rating attached. This puts real market pressure on developers to get their games rated, which in turn further enforces the standards set by the ESRB.

The ESRB's role is not to judge what you or your child should be able to view in a video or computer game, but rather to make sure that consumers are aware of the content of a particular title. This allows everyone to make more informed choices, and allows you as a parent to tell at a glance whether a game is appropriate for your child.

Under the Hood of the ESRB

The ESRB rates video and computer games and insures that when a game ships to retailers, it has the rating attached. However, the ESRB performs several other functions as well. In addition to rating game content for retail shelves, the ESRB also rates online games and websites. To make sure that the ratings the ESRB provides are objective and consistent across all the titles and sites they review, they use a unique process to assign a rating to a product.

The ESRB has over 100 trained "raters" who review game content. The raters represent a wide range of backgrounds, races, and ages and have no ties to the interactive entertainment industry. Raters include retired school principals, parents, professionals, and other individuals from all walks of life. The only common thread is that they aren't regular gamers—this allows them to review games as any consumer would at first glance. Raters are required to participate in extensive training, including a wide variety of video games and PC software products before being certified as ESRB raters.

Step #1

A game developer/publisher submits a representative sample of their work in-progress to the ESRB on three identical videotapes. This sample must contain enough game elements for someone to get a feel for the game by watching the video.

Step #2

The ESRB randomly assigns three raters to independently view the sample tapes. Each rater watches the tape and makes notes about the content they see using a set of standard descriptions established by the ESRB.

Step #3

The results of each rater's review are compared to the others. Only those descriptors that are noted by all three raters are compiled. These are then compared to the scale set up by the ESRB to determine the game's overall rating.

Step #4

The developer/publisher is informed of the rating, and given the opportunity to resubmit another set of tapes is they feel the rating is inaccurate, or if they would like to remove certain content in order to get a particular rating.

If a game is resubmitted, the second rating stands as the final rating of the game. In most cases, developers know what rating their game will get prior to submission, but the ESRB has set up the resubmission process to accommodate developers who receive unexpected results.

Once a game receives its final ESRB rating, the publisher then has the right to use one of the ESRB's trademarked icons on their packaging and advertising materials.

ESRB Rating Categories and Descriptors

Rating Categories

The ESRB has established six rating categories for video and computer games. The categories are:

EC—Early Childhood

 Titles with this rating are suitable for children 3 years of age or older and do not contain any material that parents would find inappropriate.

E—Everyone

 Contains content suitable for ages six and older. (This category was formerly K-A). These titles will appeal to people of many ages and tastes. They may contain minimal violence, some comic mischief (for example, slapstick comedy), or some crude language.

T—Teen

 Contains content suitable for ages 13 and older. Titles in this category may contain violent content, mild or strong language, and/or suggestive themes.

M—Mature

 Contains content suitable for ages 17 and older. These products may include more intense violence or language than products in the Teen category. In addition, these titles may also include mature sexual themes.

AO—Adults Only

 Contains content that is suitable only for adults. These products may include graphic depictions of sex and/or violence. Adults Only products are not intended to be sold or rented to persons under the age of 18.

RP—Rating Pending

 Although retail products usually have ratings on packaging, you may see this rating online or in advertising if a game has not yet been rated.

Of the over 5,000 titles rated by the ESRB, the breakdown by rating category is as follows:

- 3% have an EC rating
- 71% have an K-A or E rating
- 19% have a T rating
- 7% have a M rating
- Less than 1% have an AO rating

Descriptors

In addition to the rating categories, the ESRB also uses a set of descriptive terms, or "descriptors" to further enable consumers to make informed purchasing decisions. When you look on the back of a game's packaging, you may see any of the following phrases:

Violence

MILD ANIMATED VIOLENCE
Contains scenes involving characters/animated/pixilated characters in the depiction of unsafe or hazardous acts or violent situations.

MILD REALISTIC VIOLENCE
Contains scenes involving characters in the depiction of unsafe or hazardous acts or violent situations in realistic or photographic detail.

COMIC MISCHIEF
Scenes depicting activities that have been characterized as slapstick or gross vulgar humor.

ANIMATED VIOLENCE
Contains depictions of aggressive conflict involving cartoon/animated/pixilated characters.

REALISTIC VIOLENCE
Contains realistic or photographic-like depictions of body parts.

ANIMATED BLOOD AND GORE
Animated/pixilated or cartoon-like depictions of mutilation or dismemberment of body parts.

REALISTIC BLOOD AND GORE
Representations of blood and/or gore in realistic or photographic-like detail.

ANIMATED BLOOD
Animated/pixilated or cartoon-like depictions of blood.

REALISTIC BLOOD
Representations of blood in a realistic or photographic-like detail.

Language

MILD LANGUAGE
Product contains the use of the words like "damn."

STRONG LANGUAGE
Commonly referenced four-letter words that include anatomical references.

Sexual Content

SUGGESTIVE THEMES
Mild provocative references or material.
MATURE SEXUAL THEMES
Contains provocative material: including depiction of the human body either animated or photographic-like formats.
STRONG SEXUAL CONTENT
Graphic depiction of sexual behavior and/or the human form (i.e. frontal nudity) in either animated or photographic-like detail.

Early Childhood

SOME ADULT ASSISTANCE MAY BE NEEDED
READING SKILLS
FINE MOTOR SKILLS
HIGHER LEVEL THINKING SKILLS

Other Descriptors

GAMING
The depiction of betting-like behavior.
USE OF TOBACCO AND ALCOHOL
Product contains images of the use of tobacco and/or alcohol in a manner which condones or glorifies their use.
USE OF DRUGS
Product contains images of the use of drugs in a manner which condones or glorifies their use.
INFORMATIONAL
Overall content provides data, facts, resource information, reference materials or instructional text.
EDUTAINMENT
Content provides user with specific skills development or reinforcement learning within an entertainment setting. Skill development is an integral part of product.

Finding Ratings

The ESRB provides you with two kinds of visual representation in order to inform you of exactly what rating category your purchase fall into. You can find the rating category on the front of the package in the lower left or lower right corner. Descriptors are usually located in a black and white box on the back of the package.

If you can't find a rating for a product you're considering, you can call the ESRB hotline at 1-800-771-3772 to get up-to-date rating info for the game, or visit **www.esrb.org** to obtain rating information.

The combination of rating categories and descriptors will usually give you enough information about the game to make your decision. However, the ESRB recommends that you take the following steps before purchasing a game you aren't familiar with:

- First, look for ESRB ratings on the front and back of the package.
- If you can't find a rating, call 800-771-3772 or visit www.esrb.org on the Internet to obtain rating information. The 800 number and web site offer you up-to-date information on the ratings and content descriptors for every title reviewed.
- Don't forget; ESRB ratings are based only on the product's content. Ratings don't judge other qualities like gameplay or graphics.
- Examine the package carefully to see if the publisher recommends the game for particular age groups based on the skill levels required to get the most enjoyment out of the product.
- Examine the pictures and text on the product's packaging to get an idea of what the title is about.
- Ask the salesperson if you can try the product in the store before purchasing it or whether they can demonstrate it for you.
- Remember to make sure the software you're buying is compatible with your system.

Interview with Dr. Arthur Pober, ESRB Founder

Dr. Arthur Pober, founder and president of the ESRB, was gracious enough to take time out of his busy schedule and allow us to ask him a few questions about the ESRB and its role in the game industry.

Tell me about the ESRB's origins.

How did you get started?

The ESRB was founded in 1994, and grew out of the need for some sort of rating system for the growing electronic entertainment industry. In just six years, the ESRB has accomplished what the Motion Picture Association of America took decades to accomplish—we have developed a unified, industry-standard rating system that accurately reflects the content of rated products and websites.

Why does the ESRB exist?

Growth of this industry has been so rapid, that people who think of electronic entertainment as "games" don't have a clear idea of what is actually involved. It's more accurate to call this form of entertainment "interactive movies," rather than simply games. Games have gone mainstream and become part of our entertainment culture. However, until the ESRB's formation, there was no entity responsible for making sure the public could evaluate the content of this new form of entertainment independently.

Is the ESRB designed to put pressure on game publishers to remove violence and other offensive things from titles?

Not at all—our role is merely to make sure that parents can tell at-a-glance what a particular title's (or website's) content is, allowing them to make an educated decision for their child.

What similarities exist between this industry and the motion picture industry?

Several. Originally, there was no rating system for motion pictures. It took the Motion Picture Association of American (MPAA) years to develop the system. Enforcement is still an on-going issue for them, as it is for us. The two media are becoming increasingly similar, making it easy to compare the two and, more importantly, making it imperative that parents make the connection and realize the existence of the ESRB rating system and its role in helping them make informed decisions for the kids.

What is the primary difference between electronic entertainment (games) and motion pictures?

The electronic entertainment industry is rapidly changing. The changes that the Internet, new game types, and better technology have facilitated have happened very quickly. Movies, on the other hand, and our perception of their content, change less rapidly. As an example, *Midnight Cowboy*, the movie, was originally rated 'X', but was re-released recently as an 'R'-rated film. My point is that while changing perception of the public influenced the new rating, it took some time for this to happen. With games, content is changing much faster, but the public is virtually unaware of it, allowing more mature content to appear on shelves with little public fanfare.

How does the ESRB rating system work?

It's a voluntary system. The game publisher contacts us and sends in a submission form detailing the content of their game. We also receive three copies of a videotape that has the most extreme game content on them. We have over 100 trained reviewers—all non-gamers—and three are randomly assigned to view the tape separately. They watch the tape and annotate each frame using our descriptors. All three tapes are compiled, and the places where the descriptors match within five frames are added to the rating. The publisher has the chance to re-submit if they don't like the rating, or if they wish to remove content to get a specific rating. A new panel of raters is used to insure objectivity. However, this rating is the final one.

You mentioned that the system is voluntary—what's the incentive for developers to send you their games?

As a general rule, retailers don't stock un-rated games. So, if publishers want their games on retail shelves, they send us their titles for review. You will see some un-rated early childhood titles, but we are working closely with these publishers to get them rated as well. Just because it's labeled as an early childhood game, doesn't mean that parents don't need to evaluate the content pre-purchase.

Let's talk about enforcement from the retail side of things. How easy is it for children to buy games that are rated above what they should purchase?

Unfortunately, it's still too easy. As with the movie industry, it's an educational process at point of sale. We've developed training materials to help bring retail employees up to speed, but the main issue is that we've only been doing this for six years, so the awareness is just now beginning to grow. Parents need to be aware of this, and take an active role in their child's game selection.

If you could give parents just one piece of advice regarding the selection of electronic entertainment for their kids, what would it be?

Stay involved in your children's game selection—our rating system does not absolve parents of the need to evaluate content for each child. All children are different, and so are parents. Parents should make every effort to make sure a game's content matches their child's maturity level and their own parental standards as well.

79

ESRB Advisory Board

Michael Casserly
Executive Director, Council of Greater City Schools

Jeffrey I. Cole , Ph.D.
Director, Center for Communication Policy, UCLA

Charlotte Frank
Senior Vice President, Research & Development, McGraw-Hill

Mary Ellen Fise
Product Safety Director, Consumer Federation of America

Jeff Goldstein, Ph.D.
University of Utrecht, Dept. of Social & Organizational Psychology

Karen Jaffe
Executive Director, KIDSNET

Thomas F. Koerner
Deputy Executive Director,
National Association of Secondary School Principals

Lewis Lipsitt
Emeritus Professor of Psychology, Medical Science & Human
Development, Founding Director, Child Study Center Dept. of
Psychology, Brown University

Parker Page, Ph.D.
President, Children's Television Resource and Education Center

Bill Spielberg
Principal, Rogers Park Middle School

Rosemarie Truglio, Ph.D.
Director of Sesame Street Research, Children's TV Workshop

Chapter 5

PlayStation and PlayStation 2 Game Reviews

This chapter is the heart of this book. Here, you'll find a sampling of some of the most popular games for the PlayStation and PlayStation 2, including their ESRB ratings and content descriptors, as well as some information about the games. The information is presented to give you a feel for the game's content, and allow you to make educated choices about these titles.

Hot Titles

These are in-depth reviews of the most popular current titles. We felt it was important to highlight them, since these are very likely the games your children want right now.

Best Sellers

The next category of reviews are a bit shorter, but still represent a good portion of game content. The games in these reviews represent a good selection of what's available on store shelves.

Best of the Rest

These short reviews cover games that are popular on the two systems, with brief descriptions that give you a quick take on what each game is about.

Keep in mind that even if you don't find a title you're curious about in this chapter, you may see one that is similar, and it will give you some useful information that relates to the game you're looking for.

Game Review Quick Reference Chart

We've covered a lot of games in the following pages. Refer to the chart below to quickly find the title you're interested in. If you don't find it here, be sure to check out **www.marspub.com**, as we're constantly adding reviews. Finally, you can find ESRB Ratings for just about every game on the market in the Appendices.

PlayStation Titles

Hot Titles

Best Sellers

Best of the Rest

Chapter 5 • Game Reviews

The Parent's Guide Choice Award

MARS Parent's GUIDE CHOICE AWARD

As a means of identifying those offerings that contain unique educational elements, we have created the Parent's Guide Choice Award. The Award is given to those titles (on whatever gaming platform) that display imagination, creativity and ingenuity of the first order, while also offering a playing atmosphere that is educational and enriching.

The PlayStation platform is known primarily for its action and sports titles, which is why it's so hugely popular with children...and also why it's harder than usual to bestow an Award on this platform. Titles like *Crash Bandicoot* and *Motocross Madness 2* are fine examples of game design, but neither are particularly educational.

Which is why the arrival of *Harvest Moon: Back To Nature*—a PlayStation port of a classic Nintendo game—is all the more welcome. All the previous incarnations of *Harvest Moon* (which date back to 1989 on Nintendo machines) have valued nurturing over destroying and planning over plundering. Furthermore, all have also been singularly clever bits of design and programming, making the game's basic premise – to establish a working, thriving farm on a desolate lot inherited from a relative – a pleasure to play.

Since it will not be released until after this book goes to press, *Harvest Moon: Back To Nature* can only receive a provisional Parent's Guide Choice Award.

PlayStation

Hot Titles

Final Fantasy VIII

TEEN T CONTENT RATED BY ESRB

Developer: Square
Publisher: Square
Platform: PlayStation
Genre: RPG
Players: 1
ESRB Rating: Teen (13+)
ESRB Descriptors: Animated Violence, Suggestive Themes,
　　Mild Language

Final Fantasy VIII (FF8) is a fantasy roleplaying game from Squaresoft, Inc. Like the other games in the Final Fantasy series, this eighth installment involves a quest which begins as a seemingly small task, but evolves and grows until the players find themselves fighting to save the world from a great evil (in this case, a time-travelling sorceress, though that isn't revealed until late in the game).

The game's chief protagonist is Squall Leonhart, a student at an academy that trains elite mercenaries. As Squall travels throughout the world, he meets five other characters who will join him for the duration of the game, as well as a few that are temporarily playable. Rinoa Heartilly, a singer and spellcaster, acts as Squall's love interest, and this romance is at the core of the game's plot. Zell Dincht and Selphie Tilmitt, fellow students at Squall's academy, also come along for the ride once they are all assigned to their first mission. Quistis Trepe and Irvine Kinneas act as the last two of the main characters. These three women and men pair off in a series of romances during the game.

Gameplay is split between adventuring and battling. During adventuring, the player can form a party of three different characters, who travel the game world meeting various mission objectives. These aren't discrete levels; rather, the party's travels in one part of the world reveal a task that needs to be done elsewhere, and that mission will reveal more objectives elsewhere, and so on, so that the gameplay is much more story-driven than the average action game. The game spans four CD-ROMs, so there is a lot of adventuring to be done. This form of play consists mostly of exploration, with a good number of cities (safe zones, where battles don't normally occur) to explore and shop in, and a huge number of areas filled with hostile creatures. When players encounter friendly characters, they can talk to them, often engaging in long conversations where plot points and quests are revealed.

In addition to normal adventuring, there are also a number of conversations that take place between the party members themselves. This is where most of the interpersonal plot devices and romances come into play. The player will rarely control these conversations; rather, they are more like cutscenes, or short narrative films, where the plot is advanced, and the player learns more about the characters. If players, especially younger ones, don't particularly care about the complex story, these cutscenes can be skipped.

In addition to adventuring, the game features a number of battles. During battles, which can happen whenever Squall and his company are on the overland map or adventuring through a cave or other area, the characters must fight whatever beasts they encounter. These battles occur at random, and Squall and his compatriots may go through a section of a dungeon without seeing more than a half-dozen enemies; yet later, while retracing their steps, they might meet twice as many foes. The scope and variety of the enemies is incredible, with many, many distinct opponents to be encountered during the game, not including the completely unique boss, or end-of-level, creatures. The enemies are well-animated and life-like, and range from the rare human guards (encountered when you attempt to break out of prison, for instance), to the huge dragons encountered late in the game. The world itself is a seamless mixture of science fiction technology and high fantasy, so characters will sometimes find themselves battling robots at one moment only to find themselves face-to-face with hydra the next.

The combat system itself is an extension of that used in *Final Fantasy VII*. The characters are given strength, magic, speed, and other characteristics that are used to judge their effectiveness in battle. The battles are a mixture of turn-based and real-time gameplay, with each character forced to wait for their 'action bar' to fill before performing any kind of action. Of course, while the characters are waiting for their turn to act, the enemies are also sporadically attacking and performing actions. Once the players are able to act, they have a number of options. They can cast a spell, use their weapons to attack, or use an item in their inventory. In addition to these basic options, characters can use special attacks, called Limit Breaks, which become available when the character is near death. Also, the party members are able to summon creatures to aid them during battle, each of which boasts its own impressive animation. These creatures can also aid the team without being summoned, by giving the character they're bound to certain abilities that he or she may not have otherwise.

Sound complicated? It is, but most players will be able to pick up the nuances of the battle system within a few hours of gameplay. As far as the content goes, the battles are, for the most part, fairly innocuous. While the characters and enemies are rendered realistically, the attacks and such lie clearly within the realm of fantasy, with bloodless sword slashes being the most objectionable. Dead characters lie on the ground until they're resurrected by a fellow party member (if all characters die, the game ends), while enemies generally just fade away when they take a fatal amount of damage.

In addition to the adventure and battle sequences, large chunks of the game's story is revealed through computer generated imagery (CGI) sequences. These cutscenes, most of which approach the quality of a Hollywood production, are eye-candy of the first order, and will be enough to justify the purchase of the game for most gamers. Even disregarding the CGI sequences, the graphics in the game as a whole easily rank among the best available for the PlayStation.

As mentioned, the core of the game's plot revolves around the romance between Squall and Rinoa, as well as romances between the other four main characters. While the love stories might go over the heads of younger game players, teenagers might appreciate the artistry behind the story, which is more mature than those told in most games. That said, there's nothing to worry about as far as the content of the plot goes; the love stories are mostly told through inoffensive conversations, with nothing proceeding beyond the kiss that ends the game.

Final Fantasy VIII is soon to be followed by the ninth installment in the series for the PlayStation, with episodes 10 and 11 coming within the next two years for the PlayStation 2.

Chrono Cross

TEEN
T
CONTENT RATED BY
ESRB

Developer: Square Soft
Publisher: Square Electronic Arts
Platform: PlayStation
Genre: Role-Playing Game
Players: 1
ESRB Rating: Teen (13+)
ESRB Descriptors: Animated Violence, Mild Language

Hailed as one of the best games ever to appear on the PlayStation, *Chrono Cross* is the sequel to the equally lauded *Chrono Trigger* for the Super Nintendo. It doesn't deal with the characters from the first game; it is more a "spiritual continuation" of the themes that the original explored. There are some direct continuations of the first game's storyline, although knowledge of the series isn't required to play and enjoy *Chrono Cross*.

The hero of *Chrono Cross*, a man named Serge, begins his adventure after finding himself lost in a parallel universe where he supposedly died a decade before the game begins. He embarks on a quest to find the Frozen Flame, a powerful artifact that grants its wielder the ability to influence the boundary between the universes. Fortunately for Serge, he's far from alone in his quest; there are 40 separate playable characters who Serge can meet and join with. Although most traditional role-playing games stick with a core group of characters, which makes it easier to tell a coherent story, the large number of characters doesn't overwhelm *Chrono Cross*. Instead, they give the player the ability to shift between a wide range of playing styles on a whim, adding a great deal of replay value to the title. Each of the 40 characters has some form of storyline attached to him or her, with a special quest required to access their special attacks, so that players at least learn something of that character's history.

The gameplay of *Chrono Cross* is also highly innovative compared to many of the other RPGs for the PlayStation. The player can completely avoid most battles if he or she chooses to; there are no random battle sequences as in a game like *Final Fantasy VIII*. When a battle does occur, players have to manage their team's stamina, rather than wait for action

bars to fill up before attempting a movement. Each character begins a battle with seven stamina points, and certain actions take up anywhere from one to all of the points. The interesting part of this system is that characters can act whenever they have a stamina point available, removing the nagging waiting periods of traditional RPGs. Although the weapons-based combat is easy and intuitive, the most enjoyable form of battling deals with the complex magic system. The magic in *Chrono Cross* is divided into three main categories, each with two opposing specialties: Red / Blue, Black / White, and Green / Yellow.

Every character is innately powered by one of these six specialties, which affects how they deal magical damage as well as how it affects them. A Red character, for instance, deals extra damage to a Blue monster, but as a penalty, will receive more damage from Blue attacks. The opposite situation yields an opposite result: a Red character deals less damage to a Red monster, and also receives less damage from a Red attack. In addition to standard magical spells, each character is capable of using what's called a "Tech attack," a specialized move specific to that character. These are learned as the characters increase in levels, and are among the most powerful attacks in the game. These Tech attacks can occasionally be combined among characters, with two or three different characters attacking simultaneously to deal extra damage. As if that weren't enough, players can also use Summon spells to bring forth magical creatures to attack their enemies. These summoning spells are themselves bound to a certain color of magic, and can only be cast when that form of magic is the most recently used. Although the battle system sounds complex, it's actually fairly intuitive and easy to use once players get used to it.

Like most games made by Square, the storyline to *Chrono Cross* involves deeper themes than most, with love and humor being the two main elements, although there is a surprising death of a main character along the way. The bulk of these plot points play out in dialogue, but there are plenty of fully computer generated cutscenes to provide plot advancement as well as eye-candy.

Driver

Developer: Reflections
Publisher: GT Interactive
Platform: PlayStation
Genre: Driving (Arcade)
Players: 1
ESRB Rating: Teen (13+)
ESRB Descriptors: Mild Language

Driver places the player inside a '70s cop movie, complete with overpowered muscle cars and police chases through crowded city streets. The main character is Tanner, a race car driver turned undercover cop who's been ordered to infiltrate an organized crime syndicate. He does this by not only joining the syndicate, but by actually helping commit crimes. In addition, none of the other cops know he's undercover, so they chase him through the cities in which he operates. Represented in *Driver* are New York, Miami, Los Angeles, and San Francisco.

Most of *Driver's* gameplay takes place during the 'undercover' parts of the story. Tanner has to complete 10 missions in each city to earn the local Mafia's trust, and before he can advance to the next city. Most of these missions involve some kind of transportation, where Tanner has to bring a person or item from one place to another within a certain amount of time. Adding to the difficulty of the missions are the numerous cop cars that patrol the streets.

Since the time limits will generally require the player to resort to all kinds of normally illegal activity, from running red lights to driving on the sidewalk, the police will be on Tanner's tail more often than not.

The police don't have to actually see Tanner commit a crime; as he violates traffic laws, his Felony Meter will rise, which acts as a warning that cops might be about to follow him. In addition, as his car takes damage, the police will be more likely to turn on their flashers and attempt to pull him over. The cops can be outrun and outmaneuvered, but they tend to accumulate behind Tanner as he races through the city, making them difficult to evade. In addition, once one cop is on the chase, he'll radio to other police in the area, to set up roadblocks. If a cop manages to box Tanner in so that he can't speed away, or if he stops long enough near a police car, the level is failed and the player has to start over. All in all, the tension level of *Driver* is generally quite high, with most levels requiring repeated attempts to clear.

Chapter 5 • Game Reviews

In addition to the "go from point A to point B" missions, Tanner also sometimes has to disable a certain car by dealing enough damage to it, which can be difficult when the target vehicle is attempting to flee. The story branches between levels, so players will have to play the game more than once to try all of the missions. *Driver* is not an accurate driving simulation, but the driving on the whole is entertaining, with each level feeling like a car chase scene from a movie like *Bullitt* or *The French Connection*. Players can't select or modify their cars, but controls and handling are easy to learn and use. Physics in *Driver* are enjoyable rather than realistic, resulting in cars that can sustain much more damage than real cars, and also creating some interesting jumps, whether off ramps, piles of dirt, or arched roadways. The cities are populated, not only with policemen, but also with pedestrians and civilian drivers. The pedestrians will scurry out of the way when a car approaches, so they're not extra targets for overzealous players. The civilian cars are generally well-behaved, stopping at red lights and so on, but they act as if they were indestructible, refusing to get out of the way of Tanner's car even if he is approaching them head-on. All of *Driver's* cars can be damaged and will be disabled as the damage mounts.

In addition to the long-running campaign, or story mode, there are a few other short games available. Survival mode places the player's car in the middle of a city with a pack of police cars on its tail; the mission is to survive as long as possible. Cross Town Checkpoint and Trailblazer are more straight-up racing than the other modes, and the player must reach certain checkpoints scattered around a city in the fastest time possible. Cross Town Checkpoint allows the player to take any route possible, while Trailblazer forces him to stick to a certain path. Players can also simply drive through the cities, without missions, to get a feel for the quickest paths or just see the sights. Finally, the Director function allows the player to replay and edit his mission highlights, following the car via manually placed cameras, making movies that can be saved to the memory pak and shared with other game players.

Driver has been one of the most popular games for the PlayStation since its release last year, and a sequel is currently in production.

Tony Hawk's Pro Skater

Developer: Neversoft Entertainment
Publisher: Activision
Platform: PlayStation
Genre: Sports (Recreational)
Players: 4
ESRB Rating: Teen (13+)
ESRB Descriptors: Mild Language

While the sport of skateboarding might still take a back seat to soccer and other more popular sports for most young people, it's managed to stake quite a claim in video games, where the restraints of real world physics aren't a limiting factor to what a virtual skater can do. *Tony Hawk's Pro Skater* has become the most popular skateboarding game by far since its release late last year.

Rather than attempting to be a straight-up simulation of skateboarding, *Tony Hawk's Pro Skater* goes instead for a more arcade-like feel, where players attempt moves that would be dangerous, even impossible, in real life. The various modes allow for different time limits and forms of competition, but the heart of the game is in the simple yet challenging gameplay itself. Game players control a skater who has to perform various tricks and stunts to earn points. While the rudimentary tricks are easy to accomplish, the big points come from trick combinations, where players string together tricks after launching themselves into the air from various ramps. Finding the perfect place to launch into the air for maximum height and maximum time to execute combos is itself difficult, and the actual execution of these tricks requires precise timing and a lot of practice.

The most basic form of play is Free Skate. Akin to a practice mode, Free Skate allows players to choose a level and travel through it, without the hassle of a timer or a competitor. This allows the players to explore the game's nine levels without needing to race against the clock, and gives them time to practice for the tougher modes. Career mode is one of these tougher challenges, but it allows the player to unlock new levels, skateboards, and competitions. Videocassettes are the game's currency; players must collect five different videocassettes on each of the first three courses to unlock other secrets. Videocassettes are obtained in a variety of ways, from scoring a lot of points within the two-minute time limit, to finding five different letters in the level that spell out the word 'SKATE,' to finding one of the actual cassettes in the level itself.

Chapter 5 • Game Reviews

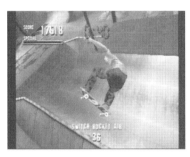

Players can also enter competitions in Career mode, where they earn points for successfully pulling off stunts, but lose points for falling. The player with the highest total points after all the racers have performed earns a gold medal in that event.

Tony Hawk's Pro Skater also has a number of mini-games for two players, most of which take place in a split-screen view. Graffiti mode is a two-minute competition where players attempt to do tricks in different parts of a level, which changes that part of the level to his color, while converting the areas that his or her opponent has tagged previously. The person with the most areas of the map in their color at the end of the two minutes wins the game. Trick Attack gives the players two minutes to battle each other, with the highest score at the end of that time winning the stage. Horse is based on the pickup basketball game of the same name, with the players taking ten-second turns in an attempt to outscore their opponent.

The action in *Tony Hawk Pro Skater* contains nothing objectionable, unless you count the helmet-less representations of ten real-world skaters (including Tony Hawk himself) performing extraordinarily dangerous maneuvers on their skateboards. The gameplay itself is rather addictive, with players coming back again and again to increase their high scores. The Mild Language rating from the ESRB likely comes from the soundtrack, which includes music from a number of rock bands, but without any really objectionable content. *Tony Hawk Pro Skater* has been ported to the Dreamcast, and a sequel is on the way for the PlayStation.

Metal Gear Solid

Developer: Konami
Publisher: Konami
Platform: PlayStation
Genre: Action
Players: 1
ESRB Rating: Mature (17+)
ESRB Descriptors: Animated Blood & Gore, Animated Violence, Mature Sexual Themes

Many game players regard *Metal Gear Solid* as one of the finest games available for the PlayStation. The story revolves around Snake Solid, a special forces operative sent to an Alaskan fortress that has been overrun by his former special op comrades, now known as the terrorist cell Fox Hound. The terrorists claim to possess enough nuclear warheads to destroy the world, and Snake must discover if this is true, all the while keeping his presence in the base a secret.

Starting the game with nothing but a pair of binoculars and a pack of cigarettes, Snake has to sneak up behind the many terrorists that prowl the facility and kill them stealthily. Unlike most action games, the emphasis here is on stealth rather than all-out gunplay, though there are still a number of fights with multiple enemies. Staying out of sight is not enough, however, as guards will be alerted to Snake's presence when he makes too much noise, or engages in a fight with nearby guards. Snake begins the game with just his fists, but he'll find a variety of weaponry as he proceeds through the multiple levels in the game.

Players control Snake from a shifting third-person perspective, usually from almost directly above, which restricts the view to a fairly small square region around Snake, though the perspective makes it easier for players to avoid guards or sneak up behind them. The radar shows a larger portion of the game world than is represented on the main screen. There is also a first-person viewpoint available for scouting out larger areas of the world, though Snake is incapable of moving or firing his gun during these times.

The plot of *Metal Gear Solid* is linear, with the player discovering new twists and turns at various points along the way. The storyline evolves with a number of cutscenes, which are rendered using the game's regular graphics and player models, instead of the beautiful (and expensive) Full Motion Video (FMV) that many games, like *Final Fantasy VIII*, employ. As the cutscenes reveal, not only are the terrorists serious in their threats, but they also possess a much more impressive weapon than a mere nuclear bomb. Snake also possesses a radio that he uses to contact various team members who guide him with either subtle or not-so-subtle hints as to where Snake should be heading next. The brevity of the game is one of its main weak points; the first time through the game takes most players around 15 hours at most, while going though a second time can take as little as three or four hours. There are no multiplayer modes to extend the life of the game.

The violence in the game is graphic, with animated blood whenever a guard is shot or killed (and guards require multiple gunshots to kill). One particularly garish scene involves an enemy being crushed to death, with his body exploding afterwards. Without a doubt, the level of blood and carnage is more extreme than in most PlayStation games. The "Mature Sexual Themes" arises from Snake's rather lewd sexual innuendoes. He propositions almost every female he encounters in some fashion. Though there is no actual nudity in the game, these conversations take place with full digital speech, so this is probably inappropriate for younger teens.

Metal Gear Solid was followed by *Metal Gear Solid: VR Missions*, another game that wasn't quite a sequel. Rather, it adds around 300 new missions without a cohesive storyline linking them together. A true sequel, *Metal Gear Solid 2: Sons of Liberty*, is set to arrive for the PlayStation 2 in late 2001 or 2002.

Resident Evil 3: Nemesis

Developer: Capcom
Publisher: Capcom
Platform: PlayStation
Genre: Action (Third Person)
Players: 1
ESRB Rating: Mature (17+)
ESRB Descriptors: Animated Blood & Gore, Animated Violence

The original *Resident Evil* used the power of the PlayStation to create an entirely new gaming genre. While it, and similar games, are classified as third person here, they're more frequently referred to as "Survival Horror" or "Panic Survival" games by video game fans. As these names would indicate, the point of *Resident Evil* was merely to survive. Placed inside a mysterious mansion filled with zombies, *Resident Evil* forced the player to balance the need to conserve ammunition and stay healthy with finding items needed to progress through the mansions.

Resident Evil 3: Nemesis is the third in the series. Somewhat confusingly, the story linking the three games jumps around a bit, which places *Nemesis* in between *Resident Evil 1* and *2* in the chronology of the series. Jill Valentine, one of the two playable characters from *Resident Evil*, reappears in *Nemesis*, and is joined by the new Carlos Oliviera character.

The plot of *Nemesis*, like the other games in the series, is somewhat complicated, but to summarize, an evil corporation has unleashed a deadly virus in the game's Raccoon City. The virus kills its victims, then transforms them into zombies hungry for human blood. Almost all of the inhabitants of Raccoon City have been transformed into zombies, which accounts for the overwhelming number of enemies that players must face. The few living residents are hiding from the carnage, and Jill and Carlos both encounter a few of these survivors during the course of the game. The game's subtitle comes from a particularly large enemy called the *Nemesis*, who pursues Jill and Carlos throughout their journeys in Raccoon City, and also acts as the game's final boss.

The player controls either Jill or Carlos at various times throughout the game; only one can be controlled at a time, as there is no multiplayer mode. The characters and monsters, which are fully 3D, move against premade backgrounds, allowing a larger amount of detail than most games are capable of. Due to the increased detail in the backgrounds, games like *Resident Evil* generally require a short loading screen in between rooms

and areas, which can be annoying. While the game offers a full view of the characters, like a Third Person game, the cameras don't move with them, and instead remain in fixed positions. The enemies are fairly slow, but they are placed in odd places, sometimes popping out when and where they are least expected, a staple of the "Panic Horror" genre. The fighting, though slow, is bloody, with bursts of blood rising when the zombies bite the character or when a character shoots an enemy.

In addition to these gameplay mechanisms, there are also a number of "Live Choices" scattered throughout the game. Essentially, these allow players to choose one action over another, with one choice changing the game for a brief time and making it impossible to choose the other option without starting a new game, or loading a saved one. This helps add a bit of replay value to the game, as players will have to play through again to see what happens when another choice is made. Finally, different modes become available after the player completes the game for the first time, with more secrets being unlocked for more efficient gameplay (less time, less damage taken, and so on).

The *Resident Evil* series of games, in addition to 1, 2, and 3, has also appeared on the Dreamcast in the form of *Resident Evil: Code Veronica*. A RE game is currently in production for the PlayStation 2 as well.

Best Sellers

Gran Turismo 2

Developer: Polyphonal Digital
Publisher: Sony Computer Entertainment
Platform: PlayStation
Genre: Driving (Simulation)
Players: 2
ESRB Rating: Everyone
ESRB Descriptors: None

One of the most in-depth driving simulations available for any console system, *Gran Turismo 2* has enough content to keep racing fans busy for quite a while. In addition to over 500 real-world, licensed cars, there is a total of 27 tracks, along with an array of gameplay modes to fiddle around with. Like most games with this many features, many of the cars are locked away, hidden until the player completes an objective that will make the car available. In this case, most of the objectives revolve around getting licenses, or car certifications, that can be quite difficult to obtain. These require driving tests, such as completing a course within a certain amount of time, or stopping your car within a certain area.

The different modes of play are also sure to increase the replay value. Arcade mode is excellent for players who dislike the difficult simulation mode. There is also rally racing, off-road racing on dirt tracks. The primary attraction of Gran Turismo for most people will be the simulation mode, where all the cars handle much as they would in real life (making some of the races quite difficult, especially on the more twisting tracks).

This difficulty can be frustrating to some players. Several of the more advanced licenses require multiple attempts to accomplish the objectives, and the higher levels of simulation mode make for extremely challenging races against excellent computer-controlled opponents. If the player is patient (and a bit stubborn), there's plenty of gameplay available here. As far as content goes, there's nothing objectionable; being a serious racing simulation, there are no pedestrians to avoid or anything like that. Crashing the car is about the worst that can happen.

Chapter 5 • Game Reviews

Syphon Filter 2

Developer: Eidetic
Publisher: 989 Studios
Platform: PlayStation
Genre: Action
Players: 2
ESRB Rating: Mature (17+)
ESRB Descriptors: Animated Blood, Animated Violence

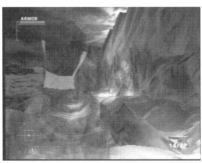

Syphon Filter 2, like its predecessor *Syphon Filter*, pits the player against an incredible number of terrorists. Playing as Gabriel Logan or his female counterpart Lian Xing, the player must save the world, yet again. In this game, an evil corporation is attempting to spread a virus (the Syphon Filter of the title), and the player's job is to thwart their plans.

Gameplay mostly consists of either Gabriel or Lian fighting their way through a mission, usually against overwhelming odds. Objectives are straight forward: avoid the enemies, prevent a bridge from being destroyed, and so on. The action is from a first or third-person perspective, with various save points scattered through the levels, making the sequel easier on the whole than the first game. The characters are well-animated, and the violence is realistic enough to earn the game a Mature rating. For example, players are encouraged to shoot their enemies in the head for quick kills.

In addition to the single-player game, there is also a split-screen Deathmatch option, where two players can fight against each other in a number of small arenas. For game players who don't have, or cannot play, online PC games, this can be a fun diversion and is a nice addition to the core gameplay, but games like *Unreal Tournament* on the PlayStation 2 and *Quake III Arena* on the PC are probably preferable for multiplayer gaming.

Legacy of Kain: Soul Reaver

Developer: Crystal Dynamics
Publisher: Eidos
Platform: PlayStation
Genre: Action (Third Person)
Players: 1
ESRB Rating: Mature (17+)
ESRB Descriptors: Animated Blood, Animated Violence

Soul Reaver, the sequel to an early PlayStation game called *Blood Omen: Legacy Of Kain*, is the tale of Raziel, a vampire that was killed by his creator, Kain, and then reanimated, so that he's probably the most undead person around. The game is primarily action-oriented, although there are portions of exploration and puzzles as well.

The action in *Soul Reaver* is from an over-the-shoulders third person perspective. The battles take place in real-time, and are fairly gruesome, with Raziel slashing at his opponents with his weapon before finally killing them with a finishing blow. This can get pretty gruesome, with enemies impaled by spears and the like. Raziel is also capable of a number of other movements, and players will find him swimming, hovering, and phasing between worlds during his adventures. The combat is necessary to Raziel's survival; his life drains slowly while he exists in the material world, and he needs to constantly recharge his energy by stealing the souls of the enemies he defeats. This constant ticking clock gives a sense of tension to the game, so that players cannot proceed too slowly.

The violence, as mentioned, is fairly graphic, and earned a Mature rating from the ESRB. While most of the enemies are of the monstrous variety, they are all rather bloodily dispatched.

Star Trek: Invasion

Developer: Warthog
Publisher: Activision
Platform: PlayStation
Genre: Driving (Arcade)
Players: 2
ESRB Rating: Everyone
ESRB Descriptors: Animated Violence

In terms of games, the *Star Trek* universe has primarily been explored by PC gamers, who have had many more games based on the popular series of TV shows than their console gaming counterparts. With the growing popularity of consoles like the PlayStation and PlayStation 2, however, some *Star Trek* games are appearing on these machines. One such game is *Star Trek: Invasion*, a space combat game where players take on the role of a Starfleet ensign who's helping Worf, a character from *Star Trek*, as the Next Generation protects the Federation and the Klingon Empire from the bizarre robotic Borg race.

The game itself is a fast-paced combat game that relies on action rather than strategy or subtlety. There are multiple ships available for the player to pilot, and a host of weapons, including the age-old photon torpedoes and phasers. The gameplay is generally fairly quick, and can often be overwhelming, with some missions facing the player off against multiple ships simultaneously. The good news is that there is plenty of content available to keep players busy: 20 levels in single-player mode, with bonus missions scattered throughout. The storyline is primarily driven by the cutscenes that play out before, during, and after each mission.

As might be expected from a game based on a television show, there's little content to worry about in terms of violence, which is why the game earned the Everyone rating from the ESRB. Ships explode when destroyed, but there's little else worthy of comment. *Star Trek* fans will appreciate the appearance of notable characters from the TV shows, such as Worf and Captain Picard, both voiced by the actors who portrayed the characters on television.

Harvest Moon: Back To Nature

Developer: Natsume
Publisher: Nintendo
Platform: PlayStation
Genre: RPG
Players: 1

Now here's a switch in console gaming: to win this game, players don't have to kill anyone, rob anyone, amass huge hoards of gold or rescue the damsel in distress. What they do have to do is...farm. There is, of course, more to *Harvest Moon* than farming: there's also ranching, roaming and (believe it or not) romancing to be done. To succeed players also need to know how to pick berries, race horses, oversee contractors and surf.

Harvest Moon began life in 1990 as a SNES title, but it was its port to the Game Boy that really made it a success. The fact that the port occurred in the mid-1990s, just at the same time that "virtual pets" were making their first big successes, was merely a lucky coincidence. This new PlayStation version (expected release November 2000), is certain to continue the tradition.

What makes *Harvest Moon* work is the smoothness and addictiveness of the gameplay and the sheer depth of the design. The game's world is heavily interactive, and each encounter, it seems, has some influence over the outcome of the game. The action mirrors life, but not too closely, and every action seems to lead logically to the next step in the process. Not the least of *Harvest Moon*'s joys is its sheer innocence.

So what, exactly, does a player do in this game? Exactly what real farmers do on their own spreads: clear, plant and till the soil; buy and plant "vegetables"; purchase and raise livestock and poultry; then sell the proceeds and hopefully make enough to keep it all going next year. It may all sound simple, but the execution proves rather difficult. More than once players will have to start over, destitute because of a lack of horses, lack of a particular herb, or they haven't talked to a mountaintop hermit.

Please note, the authors have not had a chance to review this game by press time. This review and the preliminary bestowal of the Choice Award are based on the original Nintendo 64 game.

Best of the Rest

Legend of Dragoon

> Developer: Sony Computer Entertainment
> Publisher: Sony Computer Entertainment
> Platform: PlayStation
> Genre: Role-Playing Game
> Players: 1
> ESRB Rating: Teen (13+)
> ESRB Descriptors: Animated Blood, Animated Violence

Legend of Dragoon is an RPG for the PlayStation that places the player in the role of Dart, a warrior determined to rescue his friend Shena from the Sandora Empire. Like most RPGs, his quest consists of numerous battles against fantasy-based monsters. There are a few enhancements to the combat system, in the form of Additionals, which allow Dart and his party members to link attacks together to form combinations, and the Dragoon system, which transforms the characters into a powerful Dragoon for one turn. The computer-generated cutscenes are extremely well done, but the story might move too slowly for impatient game players, especially in the early stages.

Who Wants To Be A Millionaire: 2nd Edition

> Developer: Sony Computer Entertainment
> Publisher: Sony Computer Entertainment
> Platform: PlayStation
> Genre: Puzzle
> Players: 2
> ESRB Rating: Everyone
> ESRB Descriptors: None

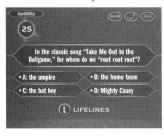

Based on the most popular PC game of 2000, as well as the TV show of the same name, *Who Wants To Be A Millionaire: 2nd Edition* is a gameshow that asks the player to answer trivia questions in order to win a virtual check for $1,000,000. Anyone familiar with the computer game or TV show will know the mechanism involved: faced with a question, players choose from among four answers. Answer correctly and the player advances to the next round. Just like the TV show, Lifelines are available to help those in need. The game can be difficult, especially for younger players, as questions (and answers) become more obscure. The two-player support is somewhat poorly implemented, as well, with long waiting periods while players complete their turns.

Spec Ops

Developer: Runecraft
Publisher: Take 2 Interactive
Platform: PlayStation
Genre: Action (First Person)
Players: 2
ESRB Rating: Teen (13+)
ESRB Descriptors: Animated Blood, Animated Violence

Another port of a PC game, *Spec Ops* is a squad-based tactical combat game, though there is only one other team member to manage here. Playing as a member of the U.S. Special Operations Ranger Corps, the player must wade through various missions, preparing their team members and formulating a basic plan of attack before each level begins. This is a value title, meaning that most stores will be carrying it for $10 or less.

Chapter 5 • Game Reviews

X-Men: Mutant Academy

Developer: Paradox
Publisher: Activision
Platform: PlayStation
Genre: Action (Fighting)
Players: 2
ESRB Rating: Teen (13+)
ESRB Descriptors: Animated Violence

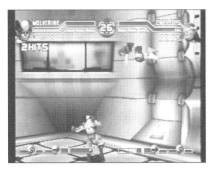

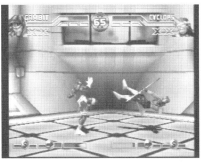

Like the *Street Fighter* games, *X-Men: Mutant Academy* is a two-dimensional, side-view fighting game. Recreating most of the popular comic book's characters, including Wolverine, Storm, Toad, Sabretooth, Professor X, along with flashy graphics and fast action, this game is sure to be popular with fans of either the comic or the recent movie. The action is like that found in comic books; laser beams, fireballs, and other sci-fi conventions all come into play, but it's never bloody. Like many 2D games, the emphasis is on "juggling" the opponent, which can take quite a bit of skill. Essentially, this consists of knocking him or her into the air and unleashing combos while they're incapacitated.

Digimon World

Developer: Bandai
Publisher: Bandai
Platform: PlayStation
Genre: Action (Fighting)
Players: 1
ESRB Rating: Teen (13+)
ESRB Descriptors: Comic Mischief

Similar to Nintendo's *Pokemon, Digimon World* lets the player collect and raise various monsters, with the goal of besting other monsters in battle. Monsters are flexible, and players direct their pet's feeding, exercise, and other needs, as well as rewarding efforts and punishing misdeeds. The virtual battles are bloodless, with the pets fighting each other with minimum player input. If your child doesn't own a Nintendo 64 or Game Boy, this might act as an acceptable *Pokemon* substitute, as it retains most of the elements that make that series of games successful, with cartoonish graphics and cute creatures.

Tekken 3

Developer: Namco
Publisher: Namco
Platform: PlayStation
Genre: Action (Fighting)
Players: 2
ESRB Rating: Teen (13+)
ESRB Descriptors: Animated Violence

Tekken 3 is one of the predescessors to *Tekken Tag Tournament*, the popular game that was available at the PlayStation 2's launch. Though *Tekken 3* is a PlayStation title, and over two years old, it's still very popular, often among the best-selling titles in any given month. The gameplay is similar to most other titles in the series, sans the tag-team mode available in *TTT*. In addition to standard fights, the game also offers Ball mode, where characters duel while trying to keep a beach volleyball in the air, and Force mode, a side-scrolling fighting mini-game along the lines of the classic Final Fight game. The violence is not overwhelming, and not as realistic as *Tekken Tag Tournament*, though there are still the brutal punches and bruising throws common to the genre.

NCAA Football 2001

Developer: EA Sports
Publisher: EA Sports
Platform: PlayStation
Genre: Sports (Major League)
Players: 4
ESRB Rating: Everyone
ESRB Descriptors: None

NCAA Football 2001 offers full representations of 140 Division 1-A and 1-AA college football teams, with an option to create a fictitious college team as well. The standard modes of play are here, including single-game Exhibition Mode, single-season Season Mode, and Dynasty mode, which lets the player play through multiple seasons back to back. In addition, there is a Situation mode that lets the player start a game with a certain amount of time left, with any number of points on the scoreboard (useful for simulating a desperation run at the end of a game when the home team is down by five points, for instance). The rather complex BCS ranking system is used, so just like in real college football, teams not only have to win, but win by large margins to earn the right to play in the Nokia Sugar Bowl or FedEx Orange Bowl.

Triple Play 2001

Developer: Treyarch
Publisher: Electronic Arts
Platform: PlayStation
Genre: Sports (Major League)
Players: 2
ESRB Rating: Everyone
ESRB Descriptors: None

EA's *Triple Play* series of baseball games has a long history on the PlayStation, with the first game in the series arriving in 1996. In addition to a simulation of a full 162 game season, plus playoffs, players can choose an abbreviated season, single game, or other types of mini-games, like the Home Run Derby. Players are given full control over their lineup, make trades, set up a starting rotation of pitchers, and even create fictitious players if they need to fill a particular gap in their team's strengths. The graphics are excellent overall, and the game sports a full MLB license.

WWF Smackdown

Developer: Yukes
Publisher: THQ
Platform: PlayStation
Genre: Action (Fighting)
Players: 4
ESRB Rating: Teen (13+)
ESRB Descriptors: Mature Sexual Themes, Animated Violence,
    Mild Language

The explosion in popularity of professional wrestling over the past few years has spread to the console gaming market, with games based on the well-known, obscure, and even fictitious wrestling leagues often ranking among the top sellers. One of the most popular of these is *WWF Smackdown*, based on the World Wrestling Federation. A wide range of wrestlers, such as The Rock, Mankind, and Stone Cold Steve Austin are modeled in the game. *Smackdown* not only simulates the action inside the ring, but also the characters' histrionics outside the ring, with players taking the 'match' backstage, and even into the parking lot outside the arena. The content is on par with any normal episode of professional wrestling, with some bruising moves and underdressed women giving the game its Mature Sexual Themes descriptor.

Army Men 3D

Developer: 3DO
Publisher: 3DO
Platform: PlayStation
Genre: Action
Players: 2
ESRB Rating: Teen (13+)
ESRB Descriptors: Animated Violence

Army Men 3D places the player in the role of Sarge, an anonymous green army man (as in the *Toy Story* films). Beyond the unique concept, the game plays much like a normal third -person game, with Sarge fighting his way through more than a dozen missions against the hated tan army men. The action isn't bloody, not that anyone would expect blood in a game featuring battles between plastic toy soldiers. There is also a two-player split screen mode for multiplayer action.

Crash Bandicoot: Warped

Developer: Naughty Dog Software
Publisher: Sony Computer Entertainment
Platform: PlayStation
Genre: Action (Platform)
Players: 1
ESRB Rating: Everyone
ESRB Descriptors: Mild Animated Violence

Crash Bandicoot, the semi-official mascot of the PlayStation, makes his third platform appearance in *Warped*, a time-traveling game where Crash and his kid sister battle Dr. Neo Cortex and another bad guy, Uka Uka, to prevent their complete galactic domination. The gameplay is true to the platform mold, with Crash and his sister rapidly moving through 35 levels of varying difficulty and format, but the game is, on the whole, easy. The slick cartoon-like graphics and colorful characters will make this game enjoyable for younger game players.

Covert Ops: Nuclear Dawn

Developer: Sugar & Rockets
Publisher: Activision
Platform: PlayStation
Genre: Action (Third Person)
Players: 1
ESRB Rating: Mature (17+)
ESRB Descriptors: Animated Violence, Animated Blood & Gore

In *Covert Ops: Nuclear Dawn*, the player controls Jack Morton, an Air Force officer charged with protecting the French Ambassador during a trip on the Blue Harvest, a military train. Terrorists hijack the train, and it's up to Jack to fight his way through the train's various cars and levels, and rescue the ambassador and regain control of the train. The viewpoint is third-person, but with set cameras instead of a flexible one that moves with the player. The violence is mostly gun-based, with Jack attempting to kill all of the terrorists he encounters, while struggling to maintain a supply of ammo. As indicated by the ESRB rating, the violence is rather graphic.

Legend of Mana

Developer: Squaresoft
Publisher: Square
Platform: PlayStation
Genre: Role-Playing Game
Players: 1
ESRB Rating: Teen (13+)
ESRB Descriptors: Mild Animated Violence, Suggestive Themes

Another RPG from the makers of the *Final Fantasy, Legend of Mana* follows a more free-flowing story-line than most console RPGs, with less emphasis on a core plot and more gameplay devoted to smaller side-quests. Whether this is good or bad depends on the player, of course; some may find the lack of a central story or main characters annoying, others will enjoy the more open-ended nature of the game. The quick-paced combat system and colorful character design is also a bonus here, with teddy bears and talking teapots, two of the notably cute cast members.

Vagrant Story

Developer: Squaresoft
Publisher: Square Electronic Arts
Platform: PlayStation
Genre: Role-Playing Game
Players: 1
ESRB Rating: Teen (13+)
ESRB Descriptors: Animated Violence

Yet another RPG from Square, *Vagrant Story* is the tale of Ashley Riot, a soldier sent to a castle to defeat the cultists that have taken control of the manor. The background story is particularly in-depth for a console title, with many twists in the plot coming at unpredictable times. The fighting system is similar to other Square RPGs, though with a bit more detail, allowing Ashley to target specific areas of the opponents' bodies. The game is fairly long, though not equal to huge games like *Final Fantasy VIII*, with about 25 hours of gameplay for experienced RPG game players.

Grind Session

Developer: Shaba Studios
Publisher: Sony Computer Entertainment
Platform: PlayStation
Genre: Sports (Recreational)
Players: 2
ESRB Rating: Everyone
ESRB Descriptors: Mild Animated Violence

Another popular skating game, *Grind Session* is from the *Tony Hawk* mold, with real-world skaters recreated in an arcadish skating world. The game is a bit easier to play than *Tony Hawk Pro Skater*, thanks to easier landings and guiding trails that show the player where some more difficult tricks can be attempted. The crashes are realistic enough, although there is no blood involved, unlike the mild spurts that accompany the worst wipe-outs in *Tony Hawk*. The level designs are also interesting, with one even allowing the game player to attempt a jump over a rail transit train.

Spyro 2: Ripto's Rage

Developer: Insomniac Games
Publisher: Sony Computer Entertainment
Platform: PlayStation
Genre: Platform
Players: 1
ESRB Rating: Everyone
ESRB Descriptors: Mild Animated Violence

Along with *Crash Bandicoot, Spyro the Dragon* is one of the PlayStation's premiere platform stars. *Ripto's Rage*, the second in the game series, pits the young dragon Spyro against the evil Ripto, a larger dragon who's been terrorizing the land of Avalar. Utilizing Spyro's fire breath, and a wide variety of special moves like swimming and climbing, the player has to explore Avalar and defeat Ripto's minions and, ultimately, Ripto himself. The character designs are friendly to younger game players, with colorful enemies and friends populating the game world.

Frogger 2

Developer: Millenium Interactive
Publisher: Hasbro Interactive
Platform: PlayStation
Genre: Action (Platform)
Players: 2
ESRB Rating: Everyone
ESRB Descriptors: None

One of the classic games from the original Atari 2600, *Frogger* has appeared on many consoles since then, and *Frogger 2* for the PlayStation is the most recent. The same gameplay from the older games exists here, with players guiding the nervous frog across crowded streets, avoiding the incessant traffic or whatever else has the potential to flatten. While the gameplay hasn't changed much, the appearance has, with this *Frogger* being a fully 3D game. The difficulty level is high, which is unfortunate because younger game players drawn to the colorful graphics might be overwhelmed by the gameplay.

Star Wars Episode I: Jedi Power Battles

Developer: LucasArts
Publisher: LucasArts
Platform: PlayStation
Genre: Action (Third-Person)
Players: 2
ESRB Rating: Teen (13+)
ESRB Descriptors: Animated Violence

One of the many games based on the popular movie *Star Wars: Episode I: The Phantom Menace, Jedi Power Battles* lets the player control one of five characters from the film, with Obi-Wan Kenobi and Qui-Gon Jinn the most popular choices. The game itself features ten levels to roam through, each with Trade Federation robots and guards to destroy, and tough battles with the film's heavy, Darth Maul. Lightsabers are the weapons of choice, so the battles are bloodless and most enemies simply explode into parts when destroyed.

Star Wars Episode I: The Phantom Menace

Developer: LucasArts
Publisher: LucasArts
Platform: PlayStation
Genre: Action (Third-Person)
Players: 1
ESRB Rating: Teen (13+)
ESRB Descriptors: Animated Violence

Based on the movie of the same name, *The Phantom Menace* is a re-creation of the recent film's plot, with players taking on the roles of Qui-Gon Jinn, Queen Amidala, Obi-Wan Kenobi, and several other characters, and battling through hordes of killer robots en route to the climactic battle with Darth Maul. The gameplay takes place from a third-person perspective, with the chosen character wielding a lightsaber or blaster rifle to protect themselves as they wander about the planet of Naboo. Like all *Star Wars* games, there's no blood or gore involved, and the majority of enemies are soulless robots.

Mega Man X4

Developer: Capcom
Publisher: Capcom
Platform: PlayStation
Genre: Action (Platform)
Players: 1
ESRB Rating: Everyone
ESRB Descriptors: Animated Blood, Animated Violence

Mega Man X4 is a side-scrolling platform game where the game player controls the aptly named Mega Man X, a robotic soldier fighting against a number of science-fictional enemies in eight different levels. Once a level is cleared, Mega Man can adapt the weaponry of the boss of that level to himself, making a new weapon to use in subsequent missions. The game can also be played through with another character, Zero, who's similar to Mega Man X, except he wields a sword in place of Mega Man's blaster. The storyline changes with each character, adding a bit of replay value. Though the game sports an Animated Blood descriptor, the gameplay is too cartoonish to be very disturbing, with flat 2D characters instead of the realistic 3D models found in many other games.

Mortal Kombat Special Forces

Developer: Midway
Publisher: Midway
Platform: PlayStation
Genre: Action (Fighting)
Players: 1
ESRB Rating: Mature (17+)
ESRB Descriptors: Animated Blood, Animated Violence

A free-movement fighting game, *Mortal Kombat Special Forces* is based on characters from the popular *Mortal Kombat* fighting games. The player controls a character and roams throughout levels, fighting through enemies with guns or bare hands. Like the other games in the series, *Mortal Kombat Special Forces* is exceptionally graphic, with enough blood and violence to earn it a Mature rating from the ESRB.

Chapter 5 • Game Reviews

Threads of Fate

> Developer: Squaresoft
> Publisher: Square Electronic Arts
> Platform: PlayStation
> Genre: Role-Playing Game
> Players: 1
> ESRB Rating: Everyone
> ESRB Descriptors: Mild Language, Animated Violence

Another RPG from Square, makers of *Final Fantasy, Threads of Fate* deals with two main characters: the shapeshifter Rue and the princess Mint. The choice of character determines the plot of the game, how certain situations will unfold, and the method of combat. Rue is capable of transforming himself into monsters that he defeats throughout his quest, while Mint uses a variety of different magical spells to battle her foes. The game world is more lighthearted than many of Square's more epic RPGs, with more charm and humor and fewer dark overtones.

Need For Speed: High Stakes

> Developer: EA Canada
> Publisher: EA Sports
> Platform: PlayStation
> Genre: Driving (Arcade)
> Players: 2
> ESRB Rating: Everyone
> ESRB Descriptors: None

Need For Speed: High Stakes is an arcadish racer that allows the player to race through a variety of challenging tracks. The basic modes are Test Drive, which allows the player to take one of the game's many cars out for a spin, and Single Race, where the player races against a number of computer opponents. Tournaments are also available, where players race through several concurrent races, which increase in difficulty and prizes. For multiplayer games, players can choose the High Stakes game, where the winner of the race actually wins the opponent's car, which is then deleted off the loser's memory card. Not as bad as losing a pink slip, but close.

Tenchu II: Birth of the Assassins

Developer: Acquire
Publisher: Activision
Platform: PlayStation
Genre: Action (Third Person)
Players: 1
ESRB Rating: Mature (17+)
ESRB Descriptors: Animated Blood & Gore, Animated Violence

In *Tenchu II*, the player controls one of three ninjas in Feudal Japan, fighting against an evil clan of ninjas, while trying to protect the lord. The action is similar to that found in *Tomb Raider*, though the emphasis is more on action than exploration. The player has to kill guards and ninjas quietly to remain undetected, and there are rewards for accomplishing missions without being detected at all. The violence is rather bloody, however, with slit throats and other gruesome methods of killing prominently featured.

Final Fantasy VII

Developer: Square
Publisher: Sony Computer Entertainment
Platform: PlayStation
Genre: Role-Playing Game
Players: 1
ESRB Rating: Teen (13+)
ESRB Descriptors: Comic Mischief, Animated Violence,
    Mild Language

One of the highest selling titles for the PlayStation so far, *Final Fantasy VII* is an RPG that places the player in control of Cloud, a sword-wielding soldier, and a ragtag group of characters that has to save the world from a megalomaniacal creature named Sephiroth. Stylistically similar to its sequel, *Final Fantasy VIII*, this game takes place in a fantasy world, with some futuristic elements thrown in as well. The impressive full-motion video sequences and length of the game (which spans three CD-ROMs) make the game attractive to most game players, especially those fond of RPGs. The Animated Violence comes into play during combat, where Cloud and his friends use their weapons and spells to defeat various enemies.

Grudge Warriors

Developer: Tempest
Publisher: Take 2 Interactive
Platform: PlayStation
Genre: Driving (Arcade)
Players: 2
ESRB Rating: Teen (13+)
ESRB Descriptors: Animated Violence

Another bargain title from Take 2, *Grudge Warriors* takes place in a futuristic setting with the player in control of a tank. The missions generally involve the player using his tank to destroy an enemy emplacement or base, or solve various puzzles. The game isn't story-driven, so there's no real 'point' to the missions other than simply defeating the enemy. Still, the action is entertaining, and the game costs less than ten dollars in most stores.

Knockout Kings 2000

Developer: EA Sports
Publisher: EA Sports
Platform: PlayStation
Genre: Sports (Major League)
Players: 2
ESRB Rating: Teen (13+)
ESRB Descriptors: Animated Violence

A boxing simulator from Electronic Arts, *Knockout Kings 2000* contains a surprising number of real-world, recognizable fighters, from the past and today. The Classic Fight mode lets the players recreate classic fights from boxing history, even such bouts as the original Ali vs. Frazier. Oscar de la Hoya, Sugar Ray Leonard, Lennox Lewis, almost all the famous professional boxers are here, except Mike Tyson. The Slugfest mode is an arcade boxing game, where players attempt to knock their opponent out without any referees or rules. The Career mode is an in-depth simulation of the sport of boxing, where a fighter can travel through a virtual career, fighting his way up through the rankings for a chance at a title fight. The violence is about as graphic as the real sport of boxing is, though players do not bleed.

Street Fighter EX2 Plus

Developer: Arika
Publisher: Capcom
Platform: PlayStation
Genre: Action (Fighting)
Players: 2
ESRB Rating: Teen (13+)
ESRB Descriptors: Animated Blood, Animated Violence

Street Fighter EX2 Plus, the awkwardly titled game from Capcom, is a translation of the traditional 2D characters of the *Street Fighter* series to a fully 3D world. All of the original characters from *Street Fighter* are present, such as Ken, Ryu, and Chun Li, but a few new additions have been made into the lineup. There isn't much in the way of modes, with most gameplay against the computer taking place in a simple last-man-standing tournament format, though two players can use the Versus mode to fight head-to-head. The violence is more extreme than in the 2D versions of the series, however, with some blood thrown into the mix as well.

Army Men: Air Attack

Developer: 3DO
Publisher: 3DO
Platform: PlayStation
Genre: Action
Players: 2
ESRB Rating: Teen (13+)
ESRB Descriptors: Animated Violence

3DO's *Army Men* franchise, based on the small green plastic soldiers, takes a small twist here, with the player not directly controlling an army man, but rather a toy helicopter. The player guides the helicopter through various missions, each of which involve defeating the evil tan soldiers. The helicopter is equipped with a machine gun, as well as secondary weapons, to directly attack the enemy, but just as often the player has to find a way to indirectly beat the opponent, utilizing the terrain or friendly units on the ground. The violence is animated, but only affects computer-generated representations of plastic toy soldiers. Real plastic army men endure far worse.

Rugrats: The Search for Reptar

Developer: N-Space
Publisher: THQ
Platform: PlayStation
Genre: Action (Platform)
Players: 1
ESRB Rating: Everyone
ESRB Descriptors: Comic Mischief

Based on the popular television show and movie, the *Rugrats* game follows the adventures of Tommy, Angelica, Spike, and the rest of the cast across 16 levels roughly based on the content of the show. There's virtually nothing objectionable here. The game is rather brief, especially for experienced game players, but younger players will take a little while longer to play through the levels. There isn't much in the way of replay value, though six of the ten levels have to be unlocked before they can be played.

Marvel Vs. Capcom

Developer: Capcom
Publisher: Capcom
Platform: PlayStation
Genre: Action (Fighting)
Players: 2
ESRB Rating: Teen (13+)
ESRB Descriptors: Animated Violence

A 2D fighting game by Capcom, *Marvel Vs. Capcom* pits the characters from the *Street Fighter* series of video games against characters from Marvel comics, such as the X-Men, Spider-Man, Captain America, and others. The combination of licenses makes the game enjoyable for comic book fans, who sometimes get the chance to use the X-Men characters in fighting games, but rarely see the other popular Marvel characters. The gameplay is classic *Street Fighter*, with two characters generally fighting on a two-dimensional plane, restricting their movement considerably compared to 3D games like Tekken. This limitation turns out to be a plus as it simplifies gameplay. The Animated Violence is not as extreme in other games, thanks to the cartoon-like characters and lack of blood.

Vanguard Bandits

Developer: Human Entertainment
Publisher: Working Designs
Platform: PlayStation
Genre: Strategy (Turn-Based)
Players: 1
ESRB Rating: Teen (13+)
ESRB Descriptors: Mild Animated Violence, Mild Language,
    Suggestive Themes

Vanguard Bandits is an anime-styled strategy game where robots fight each other in small mano-a-mano skirmishes. It also blends in a few RPG elements, with the characters earning experience from battles and gaining powers and abilities along the way. There are over 50 missions, though due to the game's branching storyline, players will have to play through the game a few times to see them all. While it might be overshadowed by more well-known strategy titles like *Final Fantasy: Tactics* or *Vandal Hearts, Vanguard Tactics* does boast some impressive elements, including some full-motion video of Japanese animation.

Reel Fishing 2

Developer: Victor Interactive
Publisher: Natsume
Platform: PlayStation
Genre: Sports (Recreational)
Players: 1
ESRB Rating: Everyone
ESRB Descriptors: None

Though they rarely make it to American shores, console fishing games are extremely popular in Japan. One of the few games that has been brought to the American market is *Reel Fishing 2,* an in-depth fishing simulation that is probably best suited towards older gamers, or teens who have a real interest in the sport of fishing. Unlike an arcade-style fishing game, *Reel Fishing 2* aims to simulate fishing as closely as possible, meaning the player is responsible for choosing the correct tackle, knowing where to cast, and how to reel in fish properly. Much like real fishing, a lot of time is spent waiting for a bite, so the action is certainly not fast-paced, but the depth of the simulation will make this a good purchase for someone who enjoys real-world fishing.

Chapter 5 • Game Reviews

119

NBA Live 2000

Developer: EA Canada
Publisher: EA Sports
Platform: PlayStation
Genre: Sports (Major League)
Players: 8
ESRB Rating: Everyone
ESRB Descriptors: None

Another in the long running *NBA Live* series, the 2000 edition sports updated rosters and some new gameplay modes. The normal modes include the single-game Exhibition match, and the Regular season mode, where players guide a basketball team through an entire regular season and into the playoffs. The 1-on-1 mode allows players to simulate a match between classic and current NBA players on an outdoor court and matchups like Magic Johnson versus Kobe Bryant are possible. The gameplay can shift from an easier arcade setting to a difficult simulation of basketball depending on the player's preference, so the game is easily adaptable to different skill levels.

Medal of Honor

Developer: Dreamworks Interactive
Publisher: Electronic Arts
Platform: PlayStation
Genre: Action (First Person)
Players: 2
ESRB Rating: Teen (13+)
ESRB Descriptors: Animated Violence

Medal of Honor is a World War II-based first-person game, placing the player in the shoes of Jimmy Patterson, a soldier picked to go behind enemy lines and perform various (and incredibly dangerous) missions. The gameplay is fairly innovative for a first-person game, with a nice mix of action and stealth required. Jimmy doesn't always shoot his opponents; sometimes, he needs to attempt to deceive German officers into believing that he's a friend, and attempt to achieve his goals without bloodshed. The graphics are very realistic, and the gameplay somewhat violent, with players being able to shoot the opponents in various body parts. Also notable is the fully original orchestral soundtrack for the game.

Koudelka

Developer: Infogrames
Publisher: Infogrames
Platform: PlayStation
Genre: Adventure
Players: 1
ESRB Rating: Mature (17+)
ESRB Descriptors: Animated Blood & Gore, Animated Violence

Koudelka takes place in a mysterious monastery, where the titular character Koudelka Iasant has been led by a disembodied voice. The main story of the game revolves around Koudelka's attempts to discover the reason that the monastery is now filled with monsters. The gameplay is similar to Capcom's *Resident Evil* series, with the requisite blood and gore of the so called "Panic Horror" titles. Two other friends accompany Koudelka as she wanders through the game: James Flattery, a bishop, and Edward Plunkett, an adventurer.

Dukes of Hazzard: Racing For Home

Developer: Sinister Games
Publisher: Southpeak Interactive
Platform: PlayStation
Genre: Driving (Arcade)
Players: 2
ESRB Rating: Everyone
ESRB Descriptors: Mild Animated Violence, Use of Alcohol & Tobacco

Featuring the characters from the TV show, including Daisy, Roscoe, and Boss Hogg, *Dukes of Hazzard: Racing For Home* is primarily a racing game, though various missions are threaded together with a storyline, something most racing games don't bother with. Not only are the Duke brothers attempting to break up some criminals that are operating in Hazzard county, but they also need to find enough money to pay off the mortgage on Uncle Jesse's farm. The missions have a variety of objectives, from racing other cars, to pulling over criminals, to collecting various items. There are a few two-player modes available, as well.

Die Hard Trilogy 2: Viva Las Vegas

Developer: N-Space
Publisher: Fox Interactive
Platform: PlayStation
Genre: Action
Players: 1
ESRB Rating: Mature (17+)
ESRB Descriptors: Animated Blood & Gore, Animated Violence

One of the more unique games for the PlayStation, *Die Hard Trilogy 2* follows the exploits of supercop John McClane as he hunts down various criminals who have escaped from a jail in Las Vegas. The gameplay is surprisingly varied for a single title, with three different segments: an arcade-style driving mode, a third-person mode, and a first-person mode. The variety offers a lot of content to a gamer, though, like the movies on which the game is based, the first and third person modes are quite violent, which explains the Mature rating from the ESRB.

A Bug's Life

Developer: Traveler's Tales
Publisher: Sony Computer Entertainment
Platform: PlayStation
Genre: Action (Third Person)
Players: 1
ESRB Rating: Everyone
ESRB Descriptors: None

A Bug's Life, based on the Disney movie of the same name, follows the ant Flik across fifteen levels as he defends his anthill from marauding grasshoppers. While categorized as an action game, there are also plenty of puzzles for Flik to solve. The action is bloodless and relatively cartoonish, given the G-rated roots of the game, and it's primarily intended for younger children.

Tomb Raider 4: The Last Revelation

Developer: Core
Publisher: Eidos
Platform: PlayStation
Genre: Action (Third Person)
Players: 1
ESRB Rating: Teen (13+)
ESRB Descriptors: Animated Blood, Animated Violence

The *Tomb Raider* series is perhaps one of the most popular among current video gamers, with four installments currently available for the PlayStation, and numbers five and six soon to appear on various platforms. The fourth and latest edition, *The Last Revelation*, features iconic Lara Croft traveling and exploring a number of levels, and she's now also capable of backtracking to previous levels when necessary. The gameplay is mostly the same as the previous games in the series, with Lara using various weapons to beat off enemies (mostly animals like wolves and bears) and jumping or swinging across ropes to reach new areas.

MediEvil 2

Developer: Sony Interactive
Publisher: Sony Computer Entertainment
Platform: PlayStation
Genre: Action (Third Person)
Players: 1
ESRB Rating: Teen (13+)
ESRB Descriptors: Animated Blood, Animated Violence

Playing as Sir Daniel Fortesque, players of *MediEvil 2* have to defeat hordes of the undead under the command of the evil wizard Zarok. Despite his plentiful weaponry, including pistols and axes and even his own arm (as in, taking his arm out of its socket and beating enemies with it), Fortesque is often overwhelmed by the sheer number of enemies, a feature common to the "Panic Horror" sub-genre. Still, the game's tone is lighthearted, despite the dark story, similar to a Tim Burton film (such as *The Nightmare before Christmas*) at times. The action can get violent, but there are plenty of puzzles to break up the combat sequences.

Chapter 5 • Game Reviews

Dino Crisis

Developer: Capcom
Publisher: Capcom
Platform: PlayStation
Genre: Action (Third Person)
Players: 1
ESRB Rating: Mature (17+)
ESRB Descriptors: Animated Blood & Gore, Animated Violence

Dino Crisis is a horror game set on an island overrun by dinosaurs, similar to the situation in the movie *Jurassic Park*. The player controls Regina, a government agent parachuted onto the island to discover the mystery behind the appearance of the dinosaurs. The game earns its Mature rating due to the fact that most of the game is spent beating off various dinosaurs in bloody and sometimes difficult conflicts. In between the fights, Regina explores the island's facilities, searching for survivors or clues.

Jeremy McGrath Supercross 2000

Developer: Iguana West
Publisher: Acclaim
Platform: PlayStation
Genre: Sports (Recreational)
Players: 2
ESRB Rating: Everyone
ESRB Descriptors: None

Jeremy McGrath Supercross 2000 is a motocross simulation, where players race against the computer or another player on a variety of dirt tracks. In the regular racing mode, game players can choose to race against the computer opponents in single races, a championship series with multiple races, or attempt to beat their own best time on one of the 16 tracks. There are also free-style modes, where the player attempts to amass points by making trick jumps on stunt courses. There is a two-player mode available for multiplayer gaming, though the split-screen is split vertically, making it difficult to see much of the racetrack, which can adversely affect the control of the bike.

Hot Shots Golf 2

Developer: Clap Hanz Limited
Publisher: Sony Computer Entertainment
Platform: PlayStation
Genre: Sports (Recreational)
Players: 4
ESRB Rating: Everyone
ESRB Descriptors: None

A fun arcade golfing game, *Hot Shots Golf 2* boasts a fairly accurate golfing game underneath the cartoonish interface and character collection. Players are ranked according to their skill in certain areas, like spinning the ball and power. There are plenty of gameplay options, from skins play to full four-round tournaments. Support for four players is a bonus, as well, if your PlayStation is equipped with a Multitap to allow this many players. A large amount of unlockable options, from new players to balls, also adds to the replay value.

Cool Boarders 4

Developer: Idol Minds Digital Entertainment
Publisher: 989 Studios
Platform: PlayStation
Genre: Sports (Recreational)
Players: 2
ESRB Rating: Everyone
ESRB Descriptors: None

Though there have been many snowboarding games for the PlayStation, the *Cool Boarders* series is perhaps the oldest of the bunch, with four games under its belt. *Cool Boarders 4*, the latest game to be released, now boasts real-world snowboarders, something the earlier games lacked, as well as a number of authentic snowboards. Gameplay is based more on arcade physics rather than 'simulation physics,' so there is an emphasis on creating combos of tricks rather than straight racing. Players can create their own snowboarder, but all wear the same outfit, so there's not much difference between stock and custom characters.

Chapter 5 • Game Reviews

Pong

Developer: Supersonic Software
Publisher: Hasbro Interactive
Platform: PlayStation
Genre: Action
Players: 2
ESRB Rating: Everyone
ESRB Descriptors: None

Perhaps the first true video game, *Pong* was originally a simple tennis-like game where players tried to knock a ball past the other player's paddle. Now, in its PlayStation incarnation, *Pong* is a rapid 3D game with the same core gameplay, but includes many new twists. There are dozens of new types of games, with each level having its own special surprises for the gamer. In addition to the single player game, there is a one-on-one mode that's just as fun as the original. There is no objectionable content, and players of the original *Pong* might enjoy the game simply for nostalgia's sake.

Tiger Woods PGA Tour 2000

Developer: EA Sports
Publisher: Electronic Arts
Platform: PlayStation
Genre: Sports (Recreational)
Players: 4
ESRB Rating: Everyone
ESRB Descriptors: None

An accurate golfing simulation in almost all aspects, *Tiger Woods PGA Tour 2000* doesn't really cater to casual duffers looking to play a short game of golf in their spare time. In addition to Tiger Woods, Lee Janzen, Mark O'Meara, and Brad Faxon are also represented in the game, which allows the multiplayer to support four players. *PGA Tour 2000* boasts the usual array of golfing mini-games, though some of the simulation elements aren't exactly true to life. For instance, players can control the flight of the ball while it's still in the air, which might be helpful for newer players, but seems to remove much of the challenge of making up for a bad shot.

Tetris Plus

Developer: Jaleco
Publisher: Jaleco
Platform: PlayStation
Genre: Puzzle
Players: 2
ESRB Rating: Everyone
ESRB Descriptors: None

While a relatively old game, having been released in 1996, *Tetris Plus* is still fairly popular among PlayStation game players. The original *Tetris* game, made for the Game Boy when it launched, was a puzzle game that challenged the player to sort and to organize falling blocks of various shapes, only to increase the pace of the game as the player cleared out previous blocks. In addition to the tried-and-true gameplay, there's also a fairly challenging puzzle mode, where the player has to clear out blocks from beneath a professor before he meets with the descending ceiling. There is, of course, a two-player mode for multiplayer *Tetris*, or two players can simply play *Tetris* on either side of the screen, without competing without each other.

Sled Storm

Developer: EA Canada
Publisher: Electronic Arts
Platform: PlayStation
Genre: Driving (Simulation)
Players: 4
ESRB Rating: Everyone
ESRB Descriptors: None

As far as driving games go, *Sled Storm* is possibly the only snowmobile racer for the PlayStation. Aiming for a balance of simulation and arcade gameplay, *Sled Storm* allows players not only to race around various courses, but also perform tricks. In fact, stunts are encouraged, and the highest scores go to racers who combine fast track times with difficult tricks. In addition to racing against the computer, there is also multiplayer support for up to 4 players at one time.

Chapter 5 • Game Reviews

Tom Clancy's Rainbow Six

Developer: Rebellion
Publisher: Red Storm Entertainment
Platform: PlayStation
Genre: Action (Tactical)
Players: 1
ESRB Rating: Teen (13+)
ESRB Descriptors: Animated Blood, Animated Violence

 Based on the popular PC game of the same name, *Tom Clancy's Rainbow Six* is a tactical squad-based first person game that puts the player in command of a squad of elite military operatives. Mission objectives range from killing terrorists to rescuing hostages. Though the controls can sometimes make the precise aiming required frustrating, there are two PlayStation-exclusive levels that might attract people who played the PC version. Like many PlayStation ports of PC first person games, *Rainbow Six* is violent, though not as violent as, for example, Unreal Tournament for the PlayStation 2.

Wild Arms 2

Developer: Contrail
Publisher: Sony Computer Entertainment
Platform: PlayStation
Genre: Role-Playing Game
Players: 1
ESRB Rating: Everyone
ESRB Descriptors: Animated Violence

One of the most recent RPGs for the PlayStation, *Wild Arms 2* concerns Ashley, the leader of a group of do-gooding mercenaries (the titular "Arms"). The adventuring portion of the game offers more interactivity than many RPGs do, with characters required to use special powers to influence the environment around them, something that is often not possible in other RPGs. The combat system is a bit easier to learn than other RPGs as well, and the level of violence isn't very high, which explains the Everyone rating from the ESRB.

Crash Team Racing

Developer: Naughty Dog Software
Publisher: Sony Computer Entertainment
Platform: PlayStation
Genre: Driving (Arcade)
Players: 4
ESRB Rating: Everyone
ESRB Descriptors: Mild Animated Violence

In addition to appearing in many platform games, Crash Bandicoot also finds time to show up in other genres, including this driving entry in *Crash Team Racing*. *CTR* is not a simulation, but it does feature many of the characters from the various Crash games. In addition to the typical race feature, there is also a single-player adventure mode, where Crash travels through various parts of the world attempting to beat enemies and bosses. The multiplayer support is particularly good, with two-player split-screen and four-player quad-split-screen modes.

Sammy Sosa High Heat Baseball 2001

Developer: Team .366
Publisher: 3DO
Platform: PlayStation
Genre: Sports (Major League)
Players: 2
ESRB Rating: Everyone
ESRB Descriptors: None

One of the many baseball games that now appear on the PlayStation annually, the *High Heat* series originated on the PC. Though last year's title had a full MLB license, this year's edition includes the additional endorsement of the Chicago Cubs' Sammy Sosa. It has all the regular options of a baseball game, with single game and full season modes available, as well as a Home Run Derby for quick throwaway games. While the full roster of Major League players is included, game players can also use the Player Edit mode to tweak the settings of each player, making superstars weaklings or no-name players powerful.

Chapter 5 • Game Reviews

Grandia

Developer: Game Arts
Publisher: Sony Computer Entertainment
Platform: PlayStation
Genre: Role-Playing Game
Players: 1
ESRB Rating: Everyone
ESRB Descriptors: Comic Mischief, Mild Animated Violence

Grandia was originally released for Sega's Saturn console in Japan over five years ago. Although many role-playing game fans hoped that it would arrive in America, the Saturn wasn't very popular in America, and *Grandia* hasn't arrived until now. Having been ported to the PlayStation, *Grandia* might not be the most graphically impressive RPG on the system, thanks mostly to its age, but the lighthearted story and characters are a change of pace from the rather serious storylines of recent games like *Final Fantasy VIII* and *Vagrant Story*. The gameplay itself is very traditional, so that any RPG fan will probably be able to wade right in and start playing with a minimum of fuss. The game revolves around two main characters, Jessie and Sue, two young childhood friends whose only hope is to travel the world and participate in adventures like Jessie's father, a famous hero. They get their wish, for the most part, and take part in a rather long quest that takes up two compact discs worth of space.

Ape Escape

Developer: Sony Computer Entertainment
Publisher: Sony Computer Entertainment
Platform: PlayStation
Genre: Action (Platform)
Players: 1
ESRB Rating: Everyone
ESRB Descriptors: Mild Animated Violence

A classic platformer for the PlayStation, *Ape Escape* puts players in the shoes of Spike, a character responsible for traveling through time in an effort to track down and capture escaped, super-intelligent monkeys that are bent on changing the history of Earth. Though it might sound convoluted, the story is primarily used as a reason to allow Spike to travel through time, which gives the various levels a good amount of variety. Spike isn't quite alone, however; his friend, the Professor, whose invention caused the monkeys to become super-smart, will help Spike through the levels and transport him to various time periods so that he can capture the monkeys, which is done with a special Time Net that instantaneously transports the simians back to the present day.

Lunar: Silver Star Story Complete

Developer: Kadokawa Shoten
Publisher: Working Designs
Platform: PlayStation
Genre: Role-Playing Game
Players: 1
ESRB Rating: Teen (13+)
ESRB Descriptors: Animated Violence, Suggestive Themes

Lunar: Silver Star Story Complete is a PlayStation version of a game that originally appeared on the archaic Sega CD console, almost a decade ago. It tells the story of Alex, a young man who wishes to become a Dragonmaster, and his quest to do so. While the gameplay is interesting, and the story is as well, the graphics are by no means the best on the PlayStation, since they are the same as they were when the game appeared early in the 1990s.

Bust A Groove 2

Developer: Enix
Publisher: Enix
Platform: PlayStation
Genre: Action
Players: 2
ESRB Rating: Everyone
ESRB Descriptors: Comic Mischief

Arguably the most interesting game genre to appear on consoles in the last few years has been the music-based dancing game. Titles like *Parappa The Rapper* and *Bust A Groove* combined the addictive elements of puzzle games and the fun characters and music of platform titles to create a new genre that has become extremely popular. *Bust A Groove 2*, the sequel to the original Bust *A Groove*, is a memory-based game that feeds the player a short string of buttons to press in time with a song being played in the background. Interestingly, the game places two characters on the game screen at the same time, who are both attempting not only to memorize and repeat the button sequences, but also to disrupt the other player, whether they're human or controlled by the computer. This is accomplished by a number of "attacks" that can break the other character's string of successful combos, but the opposing player can sometimes dodge these attacks if he or she is quick enough.

Sydney 2000

Developer: Attention To Detail
Publisher: Eidos
Platform: PlayStation
Genre: Sports (Recreational)
Players: 2
ESRB Rating: Everyone
ESRB Descriptors: None

As the name implies, *Sydney 2000* is based on the summer Olympics that were held in September of 2000 in Sydney, Australia. While it doesn't attempt to have a comprehensive catalogue of Olympic events, the 12 sports that it does emulate are well-done, although most revolve around the repetitive practice of tapping buttons on the controller as quickly as possible. The events are as follows: High Jump, Triple Jump, 100 Meter Dash, 110 Meter Hurdles, Javelin, Hammer, Skeet Shooting, 100 Meter Freestyle Swimming, 10 Meter Platform Diving, Sprint Cycling, Heavyweight Weight Lifting, and the Kayak Slalom. Needless to say, there's enough diversity among the events to keep the attention of most players for a while, but, as mentioned, the mechanics of play are hard on the hands, especially for long periods of time.

Spider-Man

Developer: Neversoft Entertainment
Publisher: Activision
Platform: PlayStation
Genre: Action (Third Person)
Players: 1
ESRB Rating: Everyone
ESRB Descriptors: Animated Violence

Spider-Man, perhaps the most popular comic book character from the large batch created in the 1960s for Marvel Comics, has recently received his own video game for the PlayStation. Taking advantage of the abilities of the console, this title gives players control over Spider-Man's wide range of abilities, from the various forms of webbing that he can emit or his power of sticking to surfaces, to the ability to crawl up and down walls and other gravity-defying stunts. The story of the game revolves around a plot by Dr. Octopus to frame Spider-Man. Spidey must not only clear his name but also avoid the police, who believe Dr. Octopus's portrayal of him as a criminal. The game contains many references to the comic books, with supervillains like Venom, Rhino, and Carnage making appearances, along with Marvel heroes like Captain America and Daredevil. The game is primarily action-oriented, however, so that a knowledge of Spider-Man's comic book history isn't necessary to enjoy the game.

Strider 2

Developer: Capcom
Publisher: Capcom
Platform: PlayStation
Genre: Action (Platform)
Players: 2
ESRB Rating: Everyone
ESRB Descriptors: Animated Violence

The original *Strider* was a success, not only in the arcades, but also on the NES and Sega's Genesis. The game's hero, Strider, leapt and slashed his way through the levels, bouncing off walls and striking down enemies with his plasma sword. The game was fairly formulaic, but some neat effects, such as reversals of gravity that allowed the player to run across the ceiling, made it popular.

Almost a decade later, *Strider 2* was released for the PlayStation. The gameplay is still much the same, with Strider roaming across 2D levels with his handy sword and leaping abilities. He has a few new tricks up his sleeve, but the game is weakened by its brevity and relative ease. Players essentially have an unlimited number of lives (they continue in the same spot where they were defeated), and the game is not very long, so that most gamers will be able to get through the whole thing within a few hours. There are a number of secrets hidden throughout, however, and the difficulty level can be increased. In addition, the game's package includes the original *Strider* on a separate CD, which most younger gamers probably haven't had the chance to play, as it is fairly old.

Ball Breakers

Developer: Lost Toys
Publisher: Take 2 Interactive
Platform: PlayStation
Genre: Action
Players: 1
ESRB Rating: Everyone
ESRB Descriptors: Animated Violence

Another budget title from Take 2 Interactive, *Ball Breakers* retails for around ten dollars. It deals with a group of androids that are imprisoned together, their feet and legs having been severed from their bodies and replaced with large balls that act as their form of locomotion.

Unfortunately, they don't have complete control over their spherical legs, which results in some bizarre movement. They cannot stop on a dime, and it takes a while to build momentum. The characters have different abilities and attributes, so that one character is fast while another is more maneuverable, and so on. The levels consist of a variety of missions, from straight-up races to more combat-oriented objectives. The robots attack each other with their fists in combat, which can make for some interesting gameplay, as players attempt to get close enough to each other without rolling past their target. There is, of course, no blood, as all the characters are robots, and the title is tame enough to earn an Everyone rating from the ESRB.

Spin Jam

Developer: Take 2 Interactive
Publisher: Take 2 Interactive
Platform: PlayStation
Genre: Puzzle
Players: 1
ESRB Rating: Everyone
ESRB Descriptors: None

Puzzle games were incredibly popular on earlier consoles, but their popularity faded in the era of more complicated games like *Tomb Raider* and *Metal Gear Solid*. There are a few puzzle games released every now and then, however, with *Spin Jam* being a notable and recent title. The gameplay is fairly complicated at first, although it becomes rather easy when a player becomes more used to it. Essentially, the point of the game is to destroy the multicolored petals on a flower by shooting like-colored bubbles at each petal, which will then burst off the flower. The bubbles are launched at the flower from a gear in the middle of the stage. The player is responsible for shooting bubbles at the gear, which, when combined in certain ways, will explode and launch nearby bubbles off the gear at the flower. The gear must be rotated so that the appropriately colored bubbles are shot in the correct direction, which can become difficult in later levels, as the flower itself begins to rotate. The pressure of the game comes from the fact that bubbles which aren't destroyed will continue to stick to the gear, causing a pileup to begin. Once the bubbles reach the edge of the screen, the player must either restart the game or use one of five continues. In addition to the single-player mode, there is a dueling mode for two players.

Lego Rock Raiders

Developer: Lego Media
Publisher: Lego Media
Platform: PlayStation
Genre: Action
Players: 2
ESRB Rating: Everyone
ESRB Descriptors: None

Lego Rock Raiders is an odd action game featuring five small Lego toys in their attempts to repair a crash-landed spaceship. In order to do so, they must first collect energy crystals spread out on the planet where they've crashed. Of course, there are numerous monsters and enemies that must be neutralized or eliminated on the 18 different levels. The characters must avoid both water (which damages them) and lava as they roam around, either on foot or in vehicles, trying to find areas to dig for energy crystals and find the teleport that ends the level. In addition to the single-player levels, there are a number of two-player missions where two players can attempt to race each other to the end of a level.

Surf Riders

Developer: Ubi Soft
Publisher: Ubi Soft
Platform: PlayStation
Genre: Sports (Recreational)
Players: 1
ESRB Rating: Everyone
ESRB Descriptors: None

Surf Riders is perhaps the only surfing game made for the PlayStation, which is odd considering the popularity of extreme sport games like *Tony Hawk Pro Skater* and any number of snowboarding and biking titles. Players attempt to gain points by doing tricks and staying aboard the wave for a long period of time. The nuances take a while to master, although the various beaches offer consistently sized waves, and there is a free playing mode available which helps beginners practice their moves on a favorite type of wave without having to worry about competition or points. The five beaches available are located in France, Japan, California, Hawaii, and Australia, with wave types ranging from large and fast to smaller, slower waves that let players perform more stunts. There is also a selection of differing boards that change the mechanics of play somewhat.

Sno Cross Championship Racing

Developer: Unique Development Studios
Publisher: Crave Entertainment
Platform: PlayStation
Genre: Driving (Simulation)
Players: 2
ESRB Rating: Everyone
ESRB Descriptors: None

Sno Cross Championship Racing is a snowmobile racing game with a number of modes of play available. The standard single race allows two players to race head-to-head in split-screen mode, and the time trial is a challenge mode in which the players attempt to beat their own best time on one of seven available tracks. Hill climbing pits the racer against a steep hill. The challenge is not just to be quick, but to survive, because a wrong turn can send the racer falling backwards. In the Championship Mode, damage sustained by the snowmobile in *Sno Cross* is permanent unless repaired, so that crashes in early races will affect the performance of the vehicle in subsequent matches. There are three tiers of racing in all, with each tier opening up more advanced vehicles and equipment, but also increasing the intelligence and speed of the computer opponents as well. In addition to all of these modes, there is a track editor that allows players to design and construct their own courses from a series of track parts.

Action Bass

Developer: Syscom Entertainment
Publisher: Take 2 Interactive
Platform: PlayStation
Genre: Sports (Recreational)
Players: 2
ESRB Rating: Everyone
ESRB Descriptors: None

Another budget title from Take 2 Interactive, *Action Bass* is available for under ten dollars in most stores. As the name suggests, it's a fishing game, and the long waits and meticulous details of more simulation-oriented fishing titles are de-emphasized in favor of more action-oriented elements. The actual fishing is mostly limited to choosing a lure and finding the areas where fish are most concentrated, and when these two factors are appropriately accounted for, fish will begin to bite. Most of the gameplay comes from the challenge mode, a fishing challenge that forces players to catch fish of a certain size in order to move on to the next tier of a tournament.

Monster Rancher Battle Card: Episode II

Developer: Tecmo
Publisher: Tecmo
Platform: PlayStation
Genre: Puzzle
Players: 1
ESRB Rating: Everyone
ESRB Descriptors: Mild Animated Violence

Monster Rancher Battle Card: Episode II is a game based on the game Monster Rancher, a Pokémon-like collectible card game where players duel with a small cadre of monsters against other players. The essential premise is that each player arranges a 50 card deck consisting of three main monsters and various other cards that are used for special attacks and abilities. The duels, that are played out against a series of computer opponents, are the core of the game, and are bound together by a story-line involving the player attempting to collect a complete set of cards in order to rescue another character from the Paradise of Monsters. The game mechanics themselves are fairly simple and easy to learn for younger players. One neat feature about the game is its ability to create new cards using other music and PlayStation CDs. Using the in-game laboratory, a player can open the PlayStation, insert a new compact disc, and receive a random (and sometimes quite powerful) card.

Iron Soldier 3

Developer: Eclipse
Publisher: Vatical Entertainment
Platform: PlayStation
Genre: Action (First Person)
Players: 2
ESRB Rating: Teen (13+)
ESRB Descriptors: Animated Violence

One of the more popular niche genres is one involving mechs, large robotic suits that a human player inhabits and controls. Games like the *Mechwarrior* series are an American example. Since it is a continuation of one of the oldest mech game series, *Iron Soldier 3* adopts most of the tried-and-true gameplay mechanics of this type of game.. The action is designed to be intense and interactive, with virtually every building being fully destructible. Although there are only three mechs available, the 24 separate missions make for a fairly long single-player game. A two-player competition is also available via a split-screen mode.

Einhander

Developer: Squaresoft
Publisher: Sony Computer Entertainment
Platform: PlayStation
Genre: Action
Players: 1
ESRB Rating: Everyone
ESRB Descriptors: Animated Violence

Although Square is a game development company best known for its many role-playing games, it occasionally produces titles from other genres, such as *Einhander*, a side-scrolling action game that puts the player in the seat of a futuristic space ship. There are a few different designs for the various ships, but the most important attribute that they all share is their ability to cannibalize the wreckage of destroyed enemies and equip themselves with the guns they find. The ships have the ability to equip these weapons facing straight forward or slightly below the ship, and can flip between the two modes at will, which adds a strategic consideration to the otherwise action-heavy game. Like many games of this genre, the difficulty can be frustratingly high at times, with most levels requiring a number of repeated attempts before the perfect scenario is achieved.

Vandal Hearts 2

Developer: Konami
Publisher: Konami
Platform: PlayStation
Genre: Strategy (Turn-Based)
Players: 1
ESRB Rating: Mature (17+)
ESRB Descriptors: Animated Blood & Gore, Animated Violence

A tactical combat fantasy game, *Vandal Hearts 2* tells the story of Joshua, a peasant who leads a group of freedom fighters against the tyrannical government. The bulk of the gameplay consists of a number of missions that take place in a 3D fighting area. Each of Joshua's fighters begins a turn with a number of action points available, and have to consider carefully how far they want to move and how they wish to attack in order not to leave themselves vulnerable. There are a variety of characters, but the three main classes are melee warriors, archers, and spellcasters. Each character begins as a basic class, but as they gain experience from battles, can choose to upgrade themselves to a higher level, allowing them access to more powerful attributes and spells. This adds to the replay value, as players can choose different classes on subsequent run-throughs of the game for a different playing experience. The combat is turn-based, with the heroes each performing an action, such as attacking or moving, and then waiting for the other side to take a turn. The goal, simply enough, is to defeat all of the characters on the other team. The game is ranked Mature by the ESRB, mainly due to the geyser of blood that bursts upwards from a defeated character. Other than that rather hyperbolic image, the content in the game is rather tame, and the strategic decisions required in combat make for some interesting puzzles.

Transformers Beast Wars: Transmetals

Developer: Genazea
Publisher: BAM Entertainment
Platform: PlayStation
Genre: Action (Fighting)
Players: 2
ESRB Rating: Teen (13+)
ESRB Descriptors: Animated Violence

Transformers Beast Wars: Transmetals is based on the television show of the same name. A fairly standard fighting game at heart, it pits the player, as one of a number of large metal dinosaur robots, against a series of opponents in one-on-one combat. Unlike most fighting games, *Transmetals* allows the combatants to roam freely through the playing field, although they will generally face each other in order to ease target acquisition. Each fighter is capable of hand-to-hand and ranged combat, but the computer will automatically determine the type of combat, depending on the distance between the fighters. In addition, each fighter is capable of transforming into a higher-power beast form, which renders them incapable of ranged combat.

Test Drive Le Mans

Developer: Eutechnyx
Publisher: Inforgrames
Platform: PlayStation
Genre: Driving (Simulation)
Players: 2
ESRB Rating: Everyone
ESRB Descriptors: None

A unique racing game, *Test Drive Le Mans* is based on endurance races, a variety of auto racing that's popular in Europe. The game has authentic cars modeled on their real-life counterparts, and two main modes of play that let the player decide how much difficulty he or she would like to experience. Amateur mode has a more arcade-like feel to it, with car damage being mostly ignored, while the professional mode is more of a straight-up simulation requiring better driving skills, with cars being gradually damaged as they make contact with the walls of the track and other cars. The championship mode of play allows the gamer to race through three seasons of increasing difficulty, with the bonus of gaining more powerful vehicles along the way. The most interesting and unique aspect of the game is the twenty-four hour endurance race of Le Mans. As you might surmise from the title, it's a twenty-four hour long endurance test, where the gamers are responsible for guiding their cars for an entire day around a racetrack, stopping every so often for fuel. Most players will probably opt to sleep rather than complete an entire endurance race, but if they attempt it, they'll notice nice touches like the accurately timed rising and setting sun.

Toy Story 2

Developer: Traveller's Tales
Publisher: Activision
Platform: PlayStation
Genre: Action (Platform)
Players: 1
ESRB Rating: Everyone
ESRB Descriptors: Animated Violence

Like the popular movie, the game adaptation of *Toy Story 2* revolves around Buzz Lightyear and his attempt to rescue the kidnapped Woody. Buzz and his compatriots (Mr. Potato Head, the Slinky dog, and the rest) travel around various miniaturized levels, attempting to find a pizza token that will let them move on to the next level. The gamers only control Buzz, however, and they wield his laser attack to fend off enemies. As an added crowd-pleaser, *Traveler's Tales*, included with the game, contain a number of cut-scenes taken directly from the film. They appear as Buzz and company progress through the missions, which parallel the same basic storyline as the movie.

Expendable

Developer: Rage Software
Publisher: Infogrames
Platform: PlayStation
Genre: Action
Players: 2
ESRB Rating: Teen (13+)
ESRB Descriptors: Animated Blood & Gore, Animated Violence

A port of a PC game, *Expendable* is a top-down action game that involves plenty of shooting. The player controls a genetically engineered soldier who can wield a large variety of weapons to defend himself from massive amounts of enemies. The weapons, with a number of power-ups, are spread out through the levels. In addition to competitive multiplayer, there is also a cooperative mode that allows two gamers to play through the single-player game simultaneously.

Parasite Eve 2

Developer: SquareSoft
Publisher: Square Electronic Arts
Platform: PlayStation
Genre: Action (Third Person)
Players: 1
ESRB Rating: Mature (17+)
ESRB Descriptors: Animated Blood & Gore, Animated Violence

Parasite Eve 2, the sequel to *Parasite Eve*, a role-playing game by SquareSoft, continues the story of Aya Brea, a young FBI agent who is somehow immune to the powers of Eve, a young woman who is infected with a bizarre kind of mitochondria that gives her strange abilities, such as the power to create vicious mutated guard creatures from normal animals. The original game, which took place in New York, saw the supposed defeat of Eve, but *Parasite Eve 2* picks up a few years afterwards, where strange creatures are appearing and mitochondria-related events have begun attracting the attention of the authorities. Stepping back into the fray, Aya must investigate the skyscraper at the epicenter of the reports and attempt to discern whether Eve is alive or not, as well as stop the mitochondria creatures.

While the first game had an intriguing combat system that was a mixture of traditional role-playing game systems and real-time combat, *Parasite Eve 2* has had its combat reworked into a fully real-time system, where Aya and her opponents are able to freely move about the game areas while fighting. Aya is capable of using a number of weapons, including guns, assault rifles, batons, and grenade launchers. In addition, as a byproduct of her natural immunity to the mitochondria, Aya is able to wield powers similar to those of Eve. Acting like magic in a traditional RPG, Aya can heal herself or use these powers to attack enemies. Aya still gains experience after battles, which translates into more abilities and health over time.

Although Aya is the centerpiece of the game, she's not without teammates who join from time to time. A variety of characters will temporarily join her as she travels through the skyscraper, acting under their own volition, with their own artificial intelligence and statistics.

Like almost all Square games, *Parasite Eve 2* contains a number of computer-generated full motion video sequences, which highlight particularly salient plot points or pivotal moments. These, and the gameplay itself, contain some rather violent and disturbing imagery at times, leading to the Mature rating from the ESRB.

Colony Wars: Red Sun

Developer: Psygnosis
Publisher: Psygnosis
Platform: PlayStation
Genre: Driving (Arcade)
Players: 1
ESRB Rating: Everyone
ESRB Descriptors: Animated Violence

Colony Wars: Red Sun is the third in a series of space combat games, where the player plays a mercenary who takes on various missions for a number of employers. As the game proceeds, more ships are unlocked, until a total of eight is reached, each distinct from the rest of the crowd (one is quite fast, one is well-armored, and so on). Since there are around 50 missions all together, taking place either near the surface of a planet or in the depths of space, there's no shortage of gameplay, even though the title is single-player only. One interesting facet to the game is the upgrading system, which requires that the player earn and spend cash on new ships and equipment, rather than having automatic upgrades. This gives players a motivation to perform well and earn as much money as possible, as the most powerful weapons and ships are, predictably, quite expensive.

PlayStation 2

A Parent's Guide to PlayStation Games went to press before the list of launch titles (games that become available the day the system is available for sale) was finalized for the PlayStation 2. Therefore, some of the PlayStation 2 games covered in this book may not be available for purchase when you read this. If a particular game interests you, however, rest assured that all of the games in this book are on track for a release before the end of 2000. This also accounts for the "Rating Pending" assigned to many of the Playstation 2 titles. They were not yet rated by the ESRB when this book was written, so you should be sure to examine the packaging, or the ESRB website, if you decide to purchase one of these titles. In addition, the maximum number of players is also unknown for some titles. This information should also be available on the box packaging.

PlayStation 2 Titles

Hot Titles

Tekken Tag Tournament

Developer: Namco
Publisher: Namco
Platform: PlayStation 2
Genre: Action (Fighting)
Players: 2
ESRB Rating: Teen (13+)
ESRB Descriptors: Animated Violence

Tekken Tag Tournament is a fighting game from Namco, and was one of the launch titles for the PlayStation 2. The only indicator from the ESRB for this game is Animated Violence, which refers to the sometimes brutal fighting moves the characters perform on each other.

The game itself plays much like any other fighting game does, with two characters slugging it out in a ring, each trying to knock out the other. *Tekken Tag Tournament* (*TTT*) adds another element to the mix with the inclusion of tag-team play, where players select two fighters and can switch between them during play. This doesn't change the actual dynamic of play very much, since the player can only control one character at a time, but it does result in longer fights.

TTT is one of the most realistic fighters ever released, with characters that appear less blocky than in games for the PlayStation. The violence is on par with professional wrestling, although there are some more extreme moves that would result in broken bones if attempted in real life and small clouds of blood are released with a successful hit. The emphasis is not on realism, however, with characters like polar bears, pandas, cyborgs, and other fantastic beings fighting it out. The game starts with just a few characters available, and as players win battles, more characters are unlocked, until a total of 36 is reached.

Unreal Tournament

Developer: Epic Games
Publisher: Infogrames
Platform: PlayStation 2
Genre: Action (First Person)
Players: 4
ESRB Rating: Rating Pending

Unreal Tournament is a port of a very popular PC title, a primarily online first person game where game players play against or with each other over the Internet. For the PlayStation 2 version, multiplayer is limited to split-screen gameplay until the Internet support for the PS2 arrives. Players can also face off against computer controlled opponents (known as bots) to practice against easier foes, or they can turn up the difficulty on the bots for a more challenging game.

There isn't much story to *Unreal Tournament*, given its primarily multiplayer background. Essentially, players are placed inside a level with anywhere from one to over two dozen opponents, and are rewarded in some fashion for killing their opponents. This is accomplished with a number of weapons, ranging from pistols and rifles to chainsaws and portable nuclear devices. Once a player dies, he or she is "respawned" at a random location on the map, free to play again until the next time they die. The PC version of this game was rated for Mature audiences by the ESRB, due to the rather extreme violence (which isn't characteristic of most console titles): opponents can be killed, decapitated, or even blown up, and large amounts of blood and flesh fly about the area.

There are a few variants of play that help keep the game fresh. The classic "Deathmatch" mode is included, of course. This is simply a free-for-all bout where all players run through the level, killing anyone they encounter, until either the time runs out or a player reaches a predetermined total of kills (or 'Frags'). Capture The Flag, another classic online game, is also included; players split into two teams, each of which must attempt to grab the opposing team's flag and return it to their own base. In Domination, another team-based game, each team tries to capture and hold various spots on the map to earn points. Assault is one of the most unique game variants, where teams take turns trying to achieve an objective. One team is generally in a defensive position on the map, while the other team attempts to break through the defense and accomplish a certain objective. While these game types are playable with one player, most game players will want to try out the split-screen multiplayer modes with friends.

Madden NFL 2001

Developer: EA Sports
Publisher: EA Sports
Platform: PlayStation 2
Genre: Sports (Major League)
Players: 8
ESRB Rating: Everyone
ESRB Descriptors: None

The series of Madden football games now spans a decade, with the earliest games in the sequence designed for the original Nintendo Entertainment System. Now, on the PlayStation 2, *Madden NFL 2001* continues the tradition with a full NFL license, including all players and teams. Utilizing the increased graphical capabilities of the PlayStation 2, *Madden NFL 2001* may be the most realistic football game ever made.

The attention to detail comes into play not only on the field, but in the many extras that are in the game as well. One of the most interesting details is the addition of real coaches, whose faces were captured using high-resolution cameras and included in the game. They prowl the sidelines, their recorded voices shouting at the referees and players from time to time. In addition to these cosmetic details, the players are faithfully reproduced from the 2000 season rosters, so new players like Ron Dayne on the Giants are included, along with all of the older players. Unlike previous versions, the individual players have been modeled to appear as similar as possible to real-world proportions, and even individual weights and running speeds are consistent with the real player.

In terms of appropriateness, there's nothing in *Madden NFL 2001* that wouldn't appear in any real football game. The game is itself presented much like a regular football broadcast, with a scoreboard, along with John Madden and Pat Summerall's recorded voices for play-by-play. The gameplay interface can be a bit complex, especially for the passing game, so very young game players might be frustrated.

Best Sellers

Dead or Alive 2: Hardcore

Developer: Team Ninja
Publisher: Tecmo
Platform: PlayStation 2
Genre: Action (Fighting)
Players: 2
ESRB Rating: Rating Pending

Although *Dead Or Alive 2* has appeared on both the Dreamcast and Japanese PlayStation 2, *Dead Or Alive 2: Hardcore* is a new, expanded edition of this fighting game for American shores. The *Dead Or Alive* games are based on hand-to-hand fighting, generally with realistic fighting moves. One of the interesting things about the game is that many of the stages are constructed so that characters can fall off the edge, landing in another fighting area below the original stage and taking a small amount of damage in the process. Like previous versions of the game, *Hardcore* includes a tag-team mode where players can use two characters in the same fight, tagging between them, and even occasionally using them both simultaneously to throw the opponent. Also included for this new version are new stages, costumes, and unlockable secrets. Though there is no blood, the brutality of the fighting is often extreme, with heads being smashed into the ground and such.

NASCAR 2001

Developer: EA Sports
Publisher: EA Sports
Platform: PlayStation 2
Genre: Driving (Simulation)
Players: 2
ESRB Rating: Everyone
ESRB Descriptors: None

NASCAR 2001 is a driving simulation from EA Sports that aims to recreate the feel of the sport of auto racing. The aim of gameplay isn't hard to guess: be the fastest car and win the race. Where *NASCAR 2001* differs from other racing simulations, though, is its realism. In addition to the large number of real-world drivers, almost 40, there are 12 real race tracks. Real announcers, teams, and sponsors are included to give the game an extra edge of authenticity. Players can choose to race in full seasons, half seasons, or, of course, just go out on a single track and let loose. The artificial intelligence is a step above most games, as well, with each car receiving a dedicated AI that models itself after its real-world counterpart, so that the Dale Earnhardt car, for example, is more aggressive than most others.

The Getaway

Developer: Studio Soho
Publisher: Sony Computer Entertainment
Platform: PlayStation 2
Genre: Driving (Arcade)
Players: 1
ESRB Rating: Rating Pending

The Getaway tells the story of Mark, a former thief whose son has been kidnapped by criminals. Though he has wished to leave his life of crime, he now finds himself forced to use his skills as a former getaway driver to find his son and rescue him The game reproduces 40 square miles of the streets of London, where most of the gameplay takes place, so that players may locate landmarks like Big Ben during their driving. The cars are based on real-life models, although the experience deals more with mission-based arcade driving rather than racing, with Mark eluding police and avoiding civilian cars by performing a number of stunts. Unlike many racing games, Mark can actually leave his car as well, to perform tasks on foot during the missions.

Rayman 2: Revolution

Developer: Ubi Soft
Publisher: Ubi Soft
Platform: PlayStation 2
Genre: Action (Platform)
Players: 1
ESRB Rating: Rating Pending

Based on the incredibly fun *Rayman 2: The Great Escape* games for the Dreamcast, Nintendo 64 and PC, *Revolution* is a PlayStation 2 exclusive game which features new levels, powers, and gameplay features. The game still revolves around Rayman, an odd cartoon character with arms and feet but no limbs connecting them to his body. His goal is to free his planet from the robotic pirates which have conquered it and enslaved the population. He roams through the levels, attempting to collect items called Lums to unlock new powers and extend his health meter. Most of the game is based on maneuvering through the hostile environments and attempting to avoid traps, although Rayman occassionally has to blast a pirate with balls of light he shoots from his hand. His movements are particularly well-animated, with Rayman turning his hair into a helicopter, climbing along walls, rolling when he hits the ground, and other motions. In portions of the game, Rayman can even climb aboard a rocket-like barrel of gunpowder and fly through the air.

Best of the Rest

NBA Live 2001

Developer: EA Canada
Publisher: Electronic Arts
Platform: PlayStation 2
Genre: Sports (Major League)
Players: 8
ESRB Rating: Rating Pending

NBA Live 2001 aims to raise the level of reality in basketball simulations. With the added power of the PlayStation 2, as well as animations that were motion-captured from star player Kevin Garnett, the game is impressive on the surface. Numerous details set it apart from games on earlier systems, such as animated crowds, reflections in the floorboards, and accurate facial details of numerous NBA players. In addition to the graphical enhancements, the audio is also improved, with more realistic conversations than in earlier installations of the game. The gameplay also includes a number of new options, which the player must unlock by performing a certain task within a game, such as getting a certain number of points with a single player or winning by a certain margin. In addition to the current NBA rosters, players will also be able to use a variety of championship teams, recreated from some of the great NBA dynasties of the past, which include specialized player models and uniforms from the era of that team.

Top Gear Dare Devil

Developer: Papaya Studios
Publisher: Kemco
Platform: PlayStation 2
Genre: Driving (Arcade)
Players: 2
ESRB Rating: Rating Pending

Top Gear Dare Devil is a city-based arcade racer that allows players to race through cities like New York, Tokyo, and London. The gameplay itself revolves around gaining "stage points" during the races, which unlock new secrets, such as additional cars and stages. The player has to avoid competitors and the cops, as well as civilian cars that are scattered throughout the courses. Two players can also challenge each other in multiplayer mode.

RC Revenge Pro

Developer: Acclaim Studios Cheltenham
Publisher: Acclaim
Platform: PlayStation 2
Genre: Driving (Arcade)
Players: 2
ESRB Rating: Rating Pending

RC Revenge Pro is a racing game with a twist; instead of dealing with real cars, it focuses on remote-controlled racers, and instead of racetracks and city streets, the courses are based on real-world environments as seen from a small vehicle's view. Although finishing first is still the priority, merely being the most skilled driver isn't always enough, as there are numerous weapons scattered around the racetracks, which are used to knock other cars out of the way or to lay a trap for the other vehicles. The courses in this edition are based around numerous themes, with a moon base, pirate ship, haunted house, and other carnival-like levels. There are around 30 vehicles in the game, each of which handles and performs in a slightly different fashion than the others.

Midnight Club

Developer: Angel Studios
Publisher: Rockstar Games
Platform: PlayStation 2
Genre: Driving (Arcade)
Players: 2
ESRB Rating: Rating Pending

A city-based arcade racer, *Midnight Club* brings the player into the world of illegal street racing. Based more on speed and fun than reality, players take one of 17 modifiable cars onto the streets of various cities to race, where they must try to avoid civilian cars, because collisions do result in damage which can eventually add up to a totaled car. As an arcade racer, players can perform jumps and other stunts with their cars, as well as search for secret passages through the city (and sometimes through the buildings themselves).

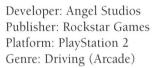

MDK2: Armageddon

Developer: Bioware
Publisher: Interplay
Platform: PlayStation 2
Genre: Action (Third Person)
Players: Unknown
ESRB Rating: Rating Pending

Although *MDK2* was released for both the Dreamcast and PC, the PlayStation 2 version is a new game, with new levels and enemies. Like the first games, however, this follows the adventures of Kurt, reluctant hero / space janitor, clad in a suit that both protects him and allows him to glide through the air in his quest to destroy aliens that are invading the earth. Also featured are Max, a four-armed dog that can conveniently wield four different weapons at once, and Dr. Hawkins, an addle-brained mad scientist type who creates new weapons by combining items he finds throughout the levels (i.e. bread in his left hand combined with a toaster in the right will pop out toast). Although the game is certainly action-oriented, with plenty of gunfights, it's not grim. In fact, it uses a goofy sense of humor that's appropriate for all ages.

Ready 2 Rumble: Round 2

Developer: Midway
Publisher: Midway
Platform: PlayStation 2
Genre: Sports (Recreational)
Players: 2
ESRB Rating: Rating Pending

A goofy, humorous boxing game, *Ready 2 Rumble: Round 2* focuses not on being a boxing simulation, but rather an arcade adaptation, complete with secret moves and verbal taunts between players. The character design is unique, as well, from the foot-wide hair of Afro Thunder to the robot fighter Robox. The practice sessions help new players get used to the fighting system, and the Championship mode is now story-based, with characters acting out rivalries on their journey towards the championship. In between fights, players can train or condition their characters, in the hopes that preparation for the next fight will make for an easier victory.

Chapter 5 • Game Reviews

NHL 2001

Developer: EA Sports
Publisher: EA Sports
Platform: PlayStation 2
Genre: Sports (Major League)
Players: 4
ESRB Rating: Rating Pending

With a full NHL license, EA Sports' *NHL 2001* continues the tradition of in depth (if at times arcadish) hockey simulations on the PlayStation 2. In addition to all the teams, including the expansion of the Minnesota Wild and Columbus Blue Jackets, as well as the players, *NHL 2001* also includes a database of player statistics and rankings from earlier NHL series, which are displayed on-screen at appropriate times in the manner of a television broadcast. If that isn't enough, the game also includes a sampling of international teams that can be paired up with the NHL franchises, or against each other. There is a large range of options that lets the players adjust the difficulty level of the game to their liking, with settings for overall speed, physics, puck movement, and a host of other variables.

Gradius III and IV

Developer: Konami
Publisher: Konami
Platform: PlayStation 2
Genre: Action
Players: Unknown
ESRB Rating: Rating Pending

Gradius III and IV isn't a new game; in fact, it's a collection of two of the most popular games of the 1980s, repackaged for the PlayStation 2. The Gradius games are side-scrolling space shooter games that pit the player, as a lone spaceship, against hordes of enemies, armed with a variety of phasers and lasers. The gameplay hasn't been changed in any way, and neither have the graphics, so while fans of the original games might enjoy having them to play, younger gamers might not be impressed with the relatively archaic visual presentation.

Oni

Developer: Bungie Games
Publisher: Rockstar
Platform: PlayStation 2
Genre: Action (Third Person)
Players: 1
ESRB Rating: Rating Pending

Oni is a third-person action game that features Konoko, a policewoman in the near future, who deals with various criminal elements that operate in her city. The perspective used allows players to use Konoko both for weapons-based combat and martial arts, so that she is capable of shooting, kicking, punching, or throwing the enemy depending on the situation at hand; Konoko can even disarm enemies by kicking the weapons out of their hands. There are around 20 levels in the game, which is also being released for the PC.

ESPN NFL Prime Time

Developer: Konami
Publisher: Konami
Platform: PlayStation 2
Genre: Sports (Major League)
Players: 4
ESRB Rating: Rating Pending

ESPN NFL Prime Time is a football game that boasts real ESPN production values as its claim to fame: Chris Berman and Tom Jackson lend their voices as the announcers, and the gameplay is interspersed with broadcast graphics, statistics, and camera angles similar to those that would be used during a televised game. *Prime Time* offers a number of modes, from the basic practice game to a full season, with playoffs. Players who enjoy following payrolls and rosters can utilize the General Manager mode, which allows them to create and guide a franchise, dealing with trades and line-ups. The player creation mode lets a gamer mold a blank slate into the perfect football pro through conditioning.

Chapter 5 • Game Reviews

ESPN International Track & Field

Developer: KCEO
Publisher: Konami
Platform: PlayStation 2
Genre: Sports (Recreational)
Players: 4
ESRB Rating: Rating Pending

While track and field events may be a niche sport in terms of real-world popularity, there have been a number of memorable video games based on the subject in the recent past, of which *ESPN International Track & Field* is the latest. Although not bearing an Olympic license, the athletes in the game are modeled on real-world Olympic athletes, with appropriate motion-captured animations for added realism. The sampling of games isn't strictly limited to classic track and field events. Although obvious choices like the 100 meter dash, pole vault, and high jump are included, less relevant t, though no less enjoyable, games are also included, such as swimming, gymnastics, and trap shooting.

ESPN NBA 2Night

Developer: Konami
Publisher: Konami
Platform: PlayStation 2
Genre: Sports (Major League)
Players: Unknown
ESRB Rating: Rating Pending

Like *ESPN NFL Prime Time, NBA 2Night* revolves around its ESPN license, with Brent Musberger and Stuart Scott providing commentary during the games. Equally important is the full NBA and player's league licenses, which allow Konami to include every player in the NBA. The play modes include a single game option, full season and post-season play, as well as an additional season of play where gamers can create their own players on the game's player editor.

Army Men Air Attack 2

Developer: 3DO
Publisher: 3DO
Platform: PlayStation 2
Genre: Action
Players: Unknown
ESRB Rating: Rating Pending

Army Men Air Attack 2, the sequel to the PlayStation game of the same name. Players control a helicopter in a variety of levels and missions, attempting to defeat the evil Tan army of plastic men and its leaders, General Plastro and Baron von Beige. The game offers five different helicopters for play, each with its own special abilities and physics of play, as well as a large amount of multiplayer support. In addition to traditional head-to-head competition, players can unite and attempt to play through single-player missions together.

Army Men Sarge's Heroes 2

Developer: 3DO
Publisher: 3DO
Platform: PlayStation 2
Genre: Action (Third Person)
Players: Unknown
ESRB Rating: Teen (13+)
ESRB Descriptors: Animated Violence

Building on the success of the Army Men franchise, 3DO has released *Sarge's Heroes 2*, a sequel to the PlayStation game of third-person perspective action games between plastic soldier toys. Since the soldiers are only two and a half inches tall, the levels are often built to emulate real-world locations from the perspective of a toy, as in the movie *Toy Story*. The characters wage battle on a kitchen table amid glasses and silverware, in a toy store, and even inside a pinball machine. There are 18 missions in all, with a variety of tactics and goals to each of them: some are simple search-and-destroy operations, while others require the player to defend an area or rescue a hostage.

World Destruction League: Thundertanks

Developer: 3DO
Publisher: 3DO
Platform: PlayStation 2
Genre: Action
Players: 1
ESRB Rating: Rating Pending

World Destruction League: Thundertanks is based on a premise that's probably discernible from the title. The player controls a tank in a gameshow-like setting, with the goal of the game being to destroy all the other tanks in the area of play. There are 11 tanks in all, each with its own unique driver and artificial intelligence. Although the game takes place in a futuristic environment, real-world locations and landmarks are visible in the various levels, including the Leaning Tower of Pisa and Moscow's St. Basil's Cathedral. There are 16 arenas in seven different cities. The game's tone isn't serious; it's more humorous than anything else, and the action is similar, with over-the-top weapons and large explosions when a tank is destroyed. This game is also available for the original PlayStation.

Disney's Dinosaur

Developer: Ubi Soft
Publisher: Disney Interactive
Platform: PlayStation 2
Genre: Adventure
Players: Unknown
ESRB Rating: Rating Pending

Based on the movie of the same name, *Dinosaur* is an adventure game that puts the players in the role of Aladar, an Iguanodon, whose way of life is disrupted by a meteor impact that brings new predators to his area. Sprinkled liberally with cutscenes from the film, *Dinosaur* contains about a dozen levels where players control one of three characters from the film, alternating between them at various times to accomplish tasks and combat vicious Velociraptors and other carnivorous beasts. Given that the movie was rated PG for "intense scenes," the material might not be appropriate for very young kids, but anyone who enjoyed the film and its characters will likely find the game appealing.

Moto GP

> Developer: Namco
> Publisher: Namco
> Platform: PlayStation 2
> Genre: Driving (Simulation)
> Players: 2
> ESRB Rating: Rating Pending

Moto GP is a game that attempts to simulate realistically the relatively obscure (in America) sport of motorcycle racing. It features a variety of real-world racetracks and bikers, and is based on the FIM Road Racing World Championship Grand Prix, a premiere motorcycle racing league. It includes the standard single-race mode, but also comes with a season simulation where players can select one of three different varieties of cycle to race on a variety of tracks in the hope of becoming the champion.

Gun Griffon Blaze

> Developer: Game Arts
> Publisher: Working Designs
> Platform: PlayStation 2
> Genre: Action (First Person)
> Players: 1
> ESRB Rating: Rating Pending

One of the two robot fighting games that arrived with the PlayStation 2's launch, *Gun Griffon Blaze* places the player inside a giant mechanized fighting robot (or 'mech'), which travels to various real-world locations (Cape Canaveral, Guam, Egypt, etc.) and destroys other mechs. The content is not overwhelmingly violent, at least for a game that's essentially all about combat. There are no human targets, and the targets of opportunity can make for some fun eye-candy, such as a fully destructible Space Shuttle. The emphasis is on quick action rather than strategic thinking, though players do sometimes need to protect other mechs or certain buildings to complete a level.

Silpheed: The Lost Planet

Developer: Game Arts
Publisher: Working Designs
Platform: PlayStation 2
Genre: Action
Players: 1
ESRB Rating: Rating Pending

Following in the footsteps of rail-driven space games like R-Type and Grades, *Silpheed: The Lost Planet* gives the player control of an advanced spaceship, and the task of destroying aliens who have invaded and lain waste to the Earth. The action is predictably fast, requiring quick reflexes both to avoid enemy fire and get in position to fire back. The game is colorful, with bright explosions and large enemies. Players get to choose the weaponry for their ship before each mission, allowing for some variation in the game experience.

Fantavision

Developer: Sony Computer Entertainment
Publisher: Sony Computer Entertainment
Platform: PlayStation 2
Genre: Puzzle
Players: 1
ESRB Rating: Rating Pending

Fantavision is one of the few puzzle games available at the launch of the PlayStation 2. The goal is to link together small colored bulbs that float through the sky and, once enough are linked together, detonate them to gain points. Larger chains of bulbs produce higher point totals, though the bulbs will gradually fade away once they're trapped, adding a time constraint to the gameplay. The action becomes fast-paced as the game proceeds, and the graphics are quite attractive, with the bulb detonations resembling a fireworks show. *Fantavision* is appropriate for all ages.

Dynasty Warriors 2

Developer: Koei
Publisher: Koei
Platform: PlayStation 2
Genre: Action (Fighting)
Players: 1
ESRB Rating: Rating Pending

An interesting take on the fighting genre, *Dynasty Warriors 2* does away with the traditional two-on-two fighting mode, instead placing the freely-roaming character in the middle of a massive battle, where he takes on enemies in weapons-based combat. Realistic human figures die (quite a bit, with some levels requiring 800 or more kills) from swords, bows, and other weapons, but the violence is rarely graphic and for the most part bloodless. Though the game focuses on the general the player controls, there is a strategic element involved in the battle, since the player's army is also involved in the battles. If a level is cleared quickly, then more friendly forces will survive to fight again in the next battle.

ESPN X-Games Snowboarding

Developer: Konami
Publisher: Konami
Platform: PlayStation 2
Genre: Sports (Recreational)
Players: 2
ESRB Rating: Rating Pending

A realistic simulation of the sport of snowboarding, *ESPN X-Games Snowboarding* features fifteen real-world boarders, along with a detailed recreation of the snowboard courses in Vermont, the last host of the winter X-Games. It follows in the footsteps of some of the more popular skateboarding games, like *Tony Hawk Pro Skater*, with open areas that allow players to board away without challenge from a clock or other competitors. There are also gameplay variations such the half-pipe and jumping competitions.

Chapter 5 • Game Reviews

Gauntlet: Dark Legacy

Developer: Midway
Publisher: Midway
Platform: PlayStation 2
Genre: Action (Third Person)
Players: 4
ESRB Rating: Teen (13+)
ESRB Descriptors: Animated Blood, Animated Violence

Mixing the action and role-playing genres, *Gauntlet: Dark Legacy* is a port of the popular arcade game. Players pick a character class from fantasy archetypes like the Wizard, Archer, or Warrior, and travel through various levels, killing beasts and finding items. The gameplay revolves around this non-stop action, and up to four players can simultaneously explore the game world, which is viewed from a top-down perspective above the playing field.

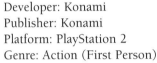

Silent Scope

Developer: Konami
Publisher: Konami
Platform: PlayStation 2
Genre: Action (First Person)
Players: 1
ESRB Rating: Rating Pending

Silent Scope is another arcade conversion, this time of a popular first person action game that lets the player emulate a sniper. Unlike conversions of PC first person games, the player in *Silent Scope* cannot control his movement, instead being moved along rails, similar to older arcade titles such as *Virtua Cop* and *Lethal Enforcers*. Like most of these types of games, the player has to fights hordes of terrorists bent on destroying the world. In this case, the player employs a sniper rifle from a great distance away. The violence may be a bit much, with realistic body damage (i.e. shooting at the head will result in an instant kill and additional points), but there's little bloodshed.

Chapter 5 • Game Reviews

SSX

Developer: EA Canada
Publisher: Electronic Arts
Platform: PlayStation 2
Genre: Sports (Recreational)
Players: 2
ESRB Rating: Rating Pending

SSX, like *ESPN X-Games Snowboarding*, is a recreation of the sport of snowboarding, but unlike the ESPN game, *SSX* (which stands for *Super Snowboard Cross*) aims for a more arcade-like feel, complete with inner-city levels and a course that's shaped like a gigantic pinball machine. Taking a page from the book of popular Midway games like *Hydro Thunder* and *Off-Road Thunder*, most of the gameplay deviates wildly from what physics would normally allow, instead placing the emphasis on gaining points and finding shortcuts through the levels. There is a variety of different play modes, and 10 different courses to explore.

FIFA 2001 Major League Soccer

Developer: EA Canada
Publisher: EA Sports
Platform: PlayStation 2
Genre: Sports (Major League)
Players: 4
ESRB Rating: Everyone
ESRB Descriptors: None

The first soccer simulation for the PlayStation 2, *FIFA 2001 MLS* includes a full license from Major League Soccer, including all the teams and the real stadiums. The graphical details, like the stadium shadows cast across players and field alike, help spice up the overall presentation. Soccer fans will enjoy the wide array of moves that the players can perform, including bicycle kicks and headers. The various modes, ranging from a single Exhibition Game to a full MLS season, also allow for increased replay value.

Kessen

Developer: Koei
Publisher: Electronic Arts
Platform: PlayStation 2
Genre: Strategy (Real-time)
Players: 1
ESRB Rating: Rating Pending

Kessen is a strategy title set in feudal Japan, and the player controls one of thirty generals through a variety of battles and missions. The emphasis is on battlefield tactics, with players deciding whether to attack, position their units, or other actions, the correct mixture of which will produce a victory. There is also strategy involved in the meta-game that ties the battles together, with decisions about diplomacy affecting the war as a whole. The gameplay features much bloodless violence, though the detailed characters and swordplay may still be too much for some.

X-Squad

Developer: EA Square
Publisher: Electronic Arts
Platform: PlayStation 2
Genre: Action (Third Person)
Players: 4
ESRB Rating: Rating Pending

X-Squad is a title that mixes the adventure, third person and RPG genres, creating a unique (and bizarre) mixture of action-oriented gunplay and team management. Ash, leader of an elite special operations squadron, has to infiltrate a quarantine city to rescue a group of scientists. Of course, there are many, many terrorists in the way that must be killed. What makes the title unique is that during the real-time battles, other team members are also making their way through the levels, independently attacking enemies and talking to civilians. Players do have a bit of control over their teammates, however, allowing for coordinated attacks on particularly tough enemies. The violence is often bloody, with realistic gunfire and well-animated enemies.

Swing Away Golf

> Developer: T&E Software
> Publisher: EA Sports
> Platform: PlayStation 2
> Genre: Sports (Recreational)
> Players: 4
> ESRB Rating: Rating Pending

The only golfing title available on PlayStation 2 at its launch, *Swing Away Golf* is more of a recreational golf game than a serious simulation. The simple interface and cartoonish characters make the game easy to play and fun to watch, while the random course generator gives the title a good amount of replay value. In addition to simple rounds, players can also choose a character and play through various ranks of golfing ability, from amateur to professional.

Theme Park Roller Coaster

> Developer: Bullfrog
> Publisher: Electronic Arts
> Platform: PlayStation 2
> Genre: Strategy (Simulation)
> Players: 1
> ESRB Rating: Rating Pending

Bullfrog's *Theme Park Roller Coaster* is an expansion of the original *Theme Park* game that was created for quite a few platforms. In it, players build, manage, and maintain a theme park. The primary task is building roller coasters, but all aspects of theme park management are controllable, from hiring the staff to placing vendor stands. In addition to building the roller coasters, the player can simulate a ride on the coaster in a first person perspective. The object of the game is to keep the park's visitors happy, by keeping lines shorts and ensuring that the park is a clean and enjoyable place.

Street Fighter EX3

Developer: Capcom
Publisher: Capcom
Platform: PlayStation 2
Genre: Action (Fighting)
Players: 2
ESRB Rating: Rating Pending

The venerable *Street Fighter* series has seen nearly two dozen versions of the game across multiple systems, but the majority of them have been 2D, flat gaming experiences, where characters could jump and move forward and backwards, but not laterally. The EX series of games has adapted the *Street Fighter* characters to a Tekken-like 3D world, and *EX3* is the first of these games to be designed for the PlayStation 2. As far as fighting games go, *EX3* is among the least realistically violent. There is still plenty of punching and kicking, but it's bloodless, and most of the characters rely on things like fireballs and cartoonish super-combos to deal damage. Also of note is the multi-player system, where players can sometimes have four different fighters on the screen at the same time.

Ridge Racer V

Developer: Namco
Publisher: Namco
Platform: PlayStation 2
Genre: Driving (Simulation)
Players: 2
ESRB Rating: Everyone
ESRB Descriptors: None

Ridge Racer V is a driving simulation, the latest in the *Ridge Racer* series of games. The game takes place completely within the fictional Ridge City, consisting of seven different tracks. Six cars are available when the game is begun, with many more hidden cars that can be unlocked as the player advances through the game. The modes include Grand Prix, consisting of a series of races against the computer; Dual mode, where two players can race head-to-head; and Time Attack, where players race for the fastest time on a given track.

Star Wars: Starfighter

Developer: LucasArts
Publisher: LucasArts
Platform: PlayStation 2
Genre: Action
Players: 1
ESRB Rating: Rating Pending

Sure to be popular with *Star Wars* fans, *Star Wars: Starfighter* is an arcadish shooter that takes place concurrently with the events in *Star Wars: Episode I: The Phantom Menace*. Taking the role of three separate characters in three different ships, the player will have to fight above the planet of Naboo to ward off the Trade Federation. The gameplay is similar to the popular *Star Wars* game *Rogue Squadron*, meaning it takes place near the surface of the planet, without heading out into space like many fans might desire. Despite that, the graphics are excellent, and the gameplay lives up to the standards that earlier *Star Wars* games have set. The content is about on par with any of the *Star Wars* movies, with the violence limited to exploding spacecraft.

Evergrace

Developer: From Software
Publisher: Acetic
Platform: PlayStation 2
Genre: Role-Playing Game
Players: 1
ESRB Rating: Rating Pending

Evergrace is an RPG from the makers of the *King's Field* games for the PlayStation. Like those games, combat takes place in real-time, with bloodless confrontations against various fantasy enemies viewed from a third-person perspective. The storyline revolves around the characters Charm and Yuterald, who begin the game far apart in the game world. The player controls each of them for short periods of time, as they proceed closer to each other, until the game's climax, where they finally meet. As usual, characters can use a variety of magical effects and physical weapons to combat enemies.

Chapter 5 • Game Reviews

Armored Core 2

Developer: From Software
Publisher: From Software
Platform: PlayStation 2
Genre: Action (Third Person)
Players: 2
ESRB Rating: Rating Pending

Another robot action game, *Armored Core 2* not only allows players to customize their mech's weaponry, but also the actual mechs themselves, by mixing and matching various body parts in order to balance the speed and power of the robot. The gameplay consists of the player taking on the various forces opposing him, with some spectacular animation and explosion effects. The gameplay is fast-paced, with the player controlling his mech from a third-person perspective.

Eternal Ring

Developer: From Software
Publisher: Agetec
Platform: PlayStation 2
Genre: Role-Playing Game
Players: 1
ESRB Rating: Rating Pending

Another RPG from the makers of the *King's Field* games, *Eternal Ring* follows those games much more closely than *Evergrace* does. While combat still takes place in real-time, the battles and exploration take place from a first-person perspective, with more rapid movement than in the *King's Field* games. The storyline follows a soldier named Cain, sent by his king to an island to explore and find the mystical Eternal ring. The battles are not incredibly violent, though the real-time, first-person perspective allows for quicker gameplay than most RPGs.

TimeSplitters

Developer: Free Radical Design
Publisher: Eidos
Platform: PlayStation 2
Genre: Action (First Person)
Players: 4
ESRB Rating: Rating Pending

Developed by members of the team that designed the enormously popular *Goldeneye* for the Nintendo 64, *TimeSplitters* is a more free-form first-person game, relying less on slow-paced stealth and more on adrenaline-fueled action. The game takes place in different eras, stretching from the 1930s to the 2030s, each consisting of its own unique enemies and weapons. The real value comes from the multiplayer game, however, with a wide variety of game modes and support for simultaneous four-player split screen action. The tone is humorous, but the action may be a bit too much for some players. There's no blood, but the detailed weapons and enemies make the violence a bit graphic.

Fusion GT

Developer: Gust
Publisher: Crave Entertainment
Platform: PlayStation 2
Genre: Driving (Arcade)
Players: 1
ESRB Rating: Rating Pending

Fusion GT is an arcadish racer, giving the player control of a variety of futuristic spacecraft as they race along a track. What makes this game different from others is that the vehicles in *Fusion GT* are capable of moving in all three dimensions, including above and below the "track," which is actually an ethereal band of energy that charges the ships. The farther a vehicle strays from the track, the slower it goes, until the racer is disqualified.

Chapter 5 • Game Reviews

Smuggler's Run

Developer: Angel Studios
Publisher: Rockstar Games
Platform: PlayStation 2
Genre: Driving (Arcade)
Players: 2
ESRB Rating: Rating Pending

As the name indicates, *Smuggler's Run* puts the player in the role of a smuggler behind the wheel of a variety of vehicles, mostly large trucks. The gameplay is similar to *Driver*, with plenty of eye-candy and obstacles to run through and over. These obstacles frequently include pedestrians, sheep, and cows, in short, innocent bystanders. As a result, there is a bit of bloodless violence in this title, as opposed to most arcade driving games, in which the pedestrians run out of the way, just like real pedestrians will. The driving isn't complicated, with most players being able to pick up the game and start playing with minimum difficulty.

Glossary

Aliasing

In sound and image generation, aliasing is the generation of a false (alias) frequency along with the correct one when doing frequency sampling. For images, this produces a jagged edge, or stair-step effect. For sound, it produces a buzz.

Alpha Channel

In computer graphics, each pixel has three channels of color information—red, green, and blue—in various bit depths. In 24-bit display graphics adapters, there are 8 bits per color per pixel, but when the card has a 32-bit bus, the additional 8 bits are used as an alpha channel to control the color information of the other 24 bits of color.

Analog

Analog technology refers to electronic transmission accomplished by adding signals of varying frequency or amplitude to carrier waves of a given frequency of alternating electromagnetic current. For example, your modem converts the digital information in your computer to analog signals for your phone line and vice versa.

Anti-Aliasing

On computer monitors the pixels themselves aren't curved, but they have to show curves. Using polygons to simulate c['aliasing, and it usually takes the form of throwing in pixels of washed-out color along the curve. This actually makes text seem a little blurred but, strangely enough, more readable.

Avatar

In online chat, your handle used to be the thing that distinguished you from everyone else. But as 3D chat worlds proliferate, the avatars are taking over. An avatar is a graphical representation that you select to stand in for you; it can look like a person, an object, or an animal. Since an avatar may look nothing like you (unless you happen to resemble a blue fish), you should choose one that fairly represents the way you'd like to be seen by the people you're chatting with.

Bandwidth

In a general sense, this term describes information-carrying capacity, or the size your (data) pipe. It can apply to telephone or network wiring as well as system buses, radio frequency signals, and monitors. Bandwidth can be measured in cycles per second, or hertz (Hz), which is the difference between the lowest and highest frequencies transmitted. It's more common to hear bandwith described in bits or bytes per second, especially when the bandwith under discussion is that of your Internet connection.

Bit

A bit is the smallest unit of data in computing, with a value of either 0 or 1. It can be prefixed with kilo- (for 1,024 bits, or 2 to the 10th power) or mega- (1,024 x 1,024 bits)—and sometimes finds its way into data transfer speeds (such as 14.4 kbps). In the console world, 8-bit, 16-bit, 64-bit, etc refers to size of the data unit the processor manipulates. The ability of the system to create color images is also measured in bits. An 8-bit graphics system can generate 256 colors (2 to the eighth power). These colors are all mixtures of Red, Green, and Blue (RGB).

Bitmap

A bitmap is a map of dots—similar to what you see when you look at a newspaper photo under a strong magnifying glass—that looks like a picture when viewed from a distance. Bitmaps come in many file formats (GIF, JPEG, TIFF, BMP, PICT, and PCX, to name a few).

If you zoom in on or try to scale up a bitmap, it will look blocky. Digital pictures that you can easily scale up (such as those created in PostScript, CorelDraw, or CAD formats) are called vector graphics.

Boss

A computer-generated and controlled opponent, usually stronger/smarter/faster/meaner than most of the other "bad guys" a player encounters in a computer/video game. Bosses generally appear close to the end of a game level or chapter.

Bus

In computer (and game console) terms, bus most commonly means the data pathway that connects the processor to memory and to other buses, such as IDE and PCI, which in turn connect to other components such as video cards, hard drives and sound cards. Faster bus speeds (measured in Mhz) means better overall performance.

Byte

One byte consists of 8 bits, much like a word is made up of several letters, which the processor treats as a single unit. Longer sequences (16 and 32 bits) are also possible.

Cache

Caches store information where your computer can get to it fast. Hard disk access is slower than RAM access, so your computer (and your console) stores information from your hard disk in faster RAM.

CD-ROM

(Compact Disc – Read Only Memory)

A compact disc used to store and play back computer data instead of digital audio. CD-ROMs can contain up to 650MB of data (though they often contain a lot less). Because of their capacity and their low cost, they have become the preferred method of distributing and installing software. Data cannot be written to a CD-ROM, though CD-ROM drives will readily Read the information they contain.

Cheat

A code, key combination, or even a program that artificially improves a player's abilities or character in a game. Cheats can either be turned on and off within a game (these are usually called codes) or the player's abilities/scores can be altered by a program that runs independently of the game program itself (also called a trainer).

CPU

The CPU is your computer's brain, taking requests from applications and then processing, or executing, them. The faster your processor (usually in Mhz), the more operations it can execute per second. The more operations you have per second, the faster things happen in your applications; games play more smoothly.

Digital

Pretty basic, and often in contrast with analog, Digital describes electronic technology that generates, stores, and processes data in terms of positive and non-positive. Positive is represented by the number 1 and non-positive by the number 0. Data transmitted or stored with digital technology is expressed as a string of 0's and 1's.

ESRB

(Electronic Software Ratings Board)

The ESRB is computer entertainment industry's ratings board. Nearly every peice of entertainment software carries a rating from the ESRB. The ratings suggest appropriate age groups and provide 'descriptors' that indicate the nature of the game's content.

First Party

In the console game publishing world, a First Party publisher is part of the company that manufactures the hardware. Nintendo develops and publishes a lot of titles for its consoles and is a First Party publisher, as are Sega and Sony (though Sony develops only a very small number of games).

First Person

In First Person games, the player sees the action and the game world from the 'characters eyes.' A First Person Shooter (FPS) is the most common type of First Person game. 'Shooters' feature lots of gunplay, and much of the outcry over violence in games is inspired by them.

Frag

An alternative verb to "kill" or "shoot to death" in multiplayer online (or networked) shooter games. Short for "fragment."

Frames Per Second (FPS)

Don't confuse this acronym (FPS) with First Person Shooter. Frames Per Second is a measurement of how quickly the computer displays game animation on your monitor or TV screen. Faster FPS translates to more real or lifelike motion. Slow FPS results in choppy or stuttering graphics and gameplay. FPS is more relevant to computer games than to console games as console developers rarely push the capabilities of the hardware to the degree that computer game developers do.

Gamer

The game player him- or herself. Also an adjective: "That's a real gamer rag," one hears said about a certain PC game magazine.

Gaming

In contrast with gaming as gambling (i.e., the Nevada Gaming Commission), gaming is the playing of computer/video games, and (as an adjective) an identifier of computer and video game-related equipment and paraphernalia, as in "gaming system," "gaming apparel" and "gaming room."

Gib

Another euphemism, a contraction of "giblet" that refers to the viscera and other remains of players' characters that splatter the floor, walls and (sometimes) ceiling after being "fragged," or killed/shot to death. In certain games one can dial in the precise amount of "gibs" one desires to experience after "fragging" an opponent.

GLOSSARY

GPU

(Graphics Processing Unit)

An additional processor dedicated to graphics. Console systems use GPUs to take the load of the main CPU and make possible 3D and high-resolution graphics. You can also think of your computer's video card as a GPU, especially if it's a 3D card.

Hit point

A unit of health, experience, strength and defensive capability, all wrapped up in one quantum. In role-playing games in particular, a player's character possesses a certain number of hit points, which gradually rises as the character becomes stronger/more experienced/etc. Also, when one loses hit points, one is said to be wounded; when one's hit points reach zero, one is unconscious, or possibly dead.

Megabyte

Mega is Greek for a million, but a megabyte actually contains 1,048,576 bytes (1,024 x 1,024 bytes).

Megahertz (MHz)

A megahertz is 1 million complete cycles per second. The unit is commonly used to measure transmission speeds of electronic devices, such as the clock speed of a CPU.

MFLOPS

(Mega-Floating Point Operations Per Second)

Another unit to measure the performance of CPUs, MFLOPS gauges the capability of your system to process with floating-point math instead of raw instructions. Floating point calculations are needed to render 3D environments. Like MHz, the more MFLOPS, the better.

MIP-Mapping

This is a complex texturing technique used for 3D animation in games and other graphically intensive applications. When scenery contains acutely angled polygons that disappear into the distance, MIP mapping mixes low- and high-resolution versions of the same texture to reduce the jagged effect and to create the illusion of depth.

MIPS

(Millions of Instructions Per Second)

MIPS is yet another unit to measure processor power. Instructions are the basic operations the processor performs at the behest of the software and shouldn't be confused with floating-point calculations.

MMOG

(Massively Multiplayer Online Game)

A new type of game made possible by the Internet, MMOGs allow thousands of players to play online together. Massively Muliplayer Online Role Playing Games (MMORPGs) are the most common MMOGs, allowing thousands of players to role play in online fantasy worlds.

MPEG (MPEG-1, MPEG-2)

(Motion Pictures Expert Group)

MPEG is the standards body that developed and approved MPEG-1 and MPEG-2, compression formats for audio and video files. MPEG-1 produces video quality far below that of standard TV. A properly compressed MPEG-2 video can be shown at near-laserdisc clarity with a CD-quality stereo soundtrack. Many recently developed video delivery mediums, such as digital satellite services and DVD, use MPEG-2. MPEG-1, layer 3 is yet another compression format known widely by the less wieldy name, MP3.

Modem

A modem modulates outgoing digital signals from your computer to analog signals for a conventional copper telephone line and demodulates the incoming analog signal and converts it to a digital signal for the digital device. The rate at which data is transferred is measured in Kbps, or Kilobits per second, with 56kbps modems very common in today's computers. Digital Subscriber Line (DSL) systems now being deployed in a number of communities provide transmission bandwidth on copper cable is in the megabit range. Don't confuse bits with bytes.

Patch

A program released by a game software company subsequent to the main release of the game itself, usually to correct bugs, correct an imbalance in the game, or in some way improve the game itself. Can be more than one.

Pixel

The smallest individual unit of a monitor or TV screen that can be assigned a color. Thay are the tiny dots that make up the picture on your display If you look very closely at your TV or computer monitor (you may need a magnifying glass), you'll see a bunch of them. The number of pixels displayed in an image is its resolution (480x600, 1024x968, etc.).

Platform

Refers to two different things: 1) the hardware environment in which a game is loaded and played (PC, PlayStation, etc.), and 2) a type of game (mostly Nintendo titles) that demands a lot of leaping to and from platforms.

RAM

(Random Access Memory)

When you run a game (on your computer or on your console), the program is pulled from its permanent storage area (the hard drive, CD-ROM or game cartridge) and moved into the RAM, where it sends requests to the CPU. Instructions sent to the CPU from RAM move much faster than if they were sent from the hard drive or cartridge. The easiest (and cheapest) way to improve system performance is to add more RAM.

Real-Time Strategy (RTS)

Think of a Real Time Strategy game as the classic 'turn-based' strategy game on caffeine. All game events occur in real-time, and all competitors perform actions simultaneously. RTSs can devolve into hyper-fast paced chaotic affairs involving too many units, or game pieces, to effectively keep track of. Never the less, RTSs are extremely popular, especially on the PC platform.

GLOSSARY

173

Resolution

A monitor's resolution is a measure of the number of pixels in the whole image. A resolution of 1,280 by 1,024 means that 1,024 lines are drawn from the top to the bottom of the screen, and each of these lines is made up of 1,280 separate pixels. Each dot, or pixel, may have any number of combinations of red, green, and blue intensities. Common resolutions in the PC world include 640 by 480 (appropriate for a 14-inch monitor), 800 by 600 (appropriate for a 15-inch monitor), 1,024 by 768 (appropriate for a 17-inch monitor), and 1,280 by 1,024.

RGB

(Red, Green, Blue)
RGB refers to the scientific colors (the additive primary colors red, green, and blue) that, when mixed together in proper amounts, can create a multitude of colors, even white. Pixels on TV sets and computer monitors are based on values of red, green, and blue.

Respawn

After being fragged (q.v.) in a multiplayer shooter game, a player is usually respawned, i.e., re-appears in the game program, usually at the "starting point."

RPG

(Role Playing Game)
Another genre most frequently found on the PC platform, RPGs are essentially computerized versions of the old 'table top' (or 'pen and paper') games such as *Dungeons & Dragons*. In an RPG, players assume the identity (or 'role') of an in-game character. Generally, the goal is to complete game objectives, such as defeating a villain, rescuing important personages, slaying dragons, etc., while simultaneously improving the character's abilities. RPGs also feature lots of interaction between players and the game's characters.

Second Party

A Second Party publisher produces games exclusively for a single game console. There are not many Second Party publishers anymore. Instead, publishers more and more are becoming Third Party publishers as they try to get their products on as many different platforms as possible.

S-Video

(Super Video)
A video standard that generates roughly 400 horizontal lines on your screen or monitor. RGB is better, but S-Video is superior to regular TV. If your TV has S-Video inputs, the just released PlayStation2 supports it.

Third Party

Third Party publishers publish software for game consoles they did not manufacture. Console manufacturers rely heavily on these companies to fill out the availability of games in the market, and to push the technological development of software for the system. No console can succeed in the market without solid contributions from Third Party publishers.

Turn Based

This is a term used to describe how a game is played. Familiar turn based games are Monopoly, or Chess, where players take turns performing actions. In computer and video games, many strategy and RPG games use some form of turn system, especially to resolve combat.

ESRB Ratings, By Platform and Game Title

The ESRB ratings listed below are by no means complete. We've filtered out a number of 'older' titles and only included PlayStation and PlayStation 2 platforms. Nevertheless, the list here is extensive. If you don't find a game you're interested in, be sure to check out the ESRB's data at their website, www.esrb.org

PlayStation Games

Game Title	Publisher	Rating	Descriptor
102 Dalmations Puppies to the Rescue	Eidos Interactive	Everyone	No Descriptors
2 Extreme	Sony Interactive - Foster City	Kids To Adults	No Descriptors
3D Baseball	Crystal Dynamics	Kids To Adults	No Descriptors
3D Fighter Maker	ASCII	Teen (13+)	Animated Violence
3extreme	989 Studios	Everyone	No Descriptors
40 Winks	GT Interactive	Everyone	Animated Violence
A Bugs Life	989 Studios	Everyone	No Descriptors
Ace Combat 2	Namco Hometek	Kids To Adults	Animated Violence
Ace Combat 3 Electrosphere	Namco Hometek	Everyone	Animated Violence
Action Bass	Take 2 Interactive Software, Inc.	Everyone	No Descriptors
Action Man Mission Xtreme Psx	Hasbro Interactive	Teen (13+)	Mild Animated Violence
Activision Classics	Activision	Everyone	Mild Animated Violence
Adidas Power Soccer 98	Psygnosis	Everyone	No Descriptors
Adventures of Lomax in Lemingland	Psygnosis	Kids To Adults	No Descriptors
Agent Armstrong PSX	GT Interactive	Teen (13+)	Animated Violence
Akuji the Heartless	Crystal Dynamics	Teen (13+)	Animated Blood & Gore, Animated Violence
Alexi Lalas International Soccer	Take 2 Interactive Software, Inc.	Everyone	No Descriptors
Alien Resurrection	Fox Interactive	Mature (17+)	Animated Blood & Gore, Animated Violence
All Star Baseball 97 Featuring Frank Thomas	Acclaim	Kids To Adults	No Descriptors
All Star Tennis 99	Ubi Soft	Everyone	Mild Animated Violence
Alundra	Working Design	Teen (13+)	Comic Mischief, Mild Animated Violence
Alundra 2	Activision	Teen (13+)	Mild Animated Violence
American Deer Hunter	Interplay Prods.	Teen (13+)	Animated Violence
Andretti Racing 97	Electronic Arts	Kids To Adults	No Descriptors
Animaniacs Ten Pin Alley	ASC American Softworks	Everyone	No Descriptors
Ape Escape	Sony Interactive - Foster City	Everyone	Mild Animated Violence
Apocalypse	Activision	Teen (13+)	Animated Blood & Gore, Animated Violence, Mild Language
Arcade Party Pack	Midway Home Entertainment	Teen (13+)	Animated Blood, Animated Violence
Arcade's Greatest Hits The Atari Collection 2	Midway Home Entertainment	Everyone	Animated Violence
Area 51	Atari Games/Williams	Mature (17+)	Realistic Violence
Armed	Interplay Prods.	Teen (13+)	Animated Violence
Armored Core	Sony Computer Entertainment	Teen (13+)	Animated Violence
Armored Core Master of Arena	AGETEC,Inc.	Teen (13+)	Animated Violence
Armored Core Project Phantasma	ASCII	Teen (13+)	Animated Violence
Armorines Project S W A R M	Acclaim	Teen (13+)	Animated Blood, Animated Violence
Army Men 3D	3 DO	Teen (13+)	Animated Violence
Army Men Air Attack	3 DO	Teen (13+)	Animated Violence
Army Men Sarge's Heroes	3 DO	Teen (13+)	Animated Violence
Army Men Sarge's Heroes 2	3 DO	Teen (13+)	Animated Violence
Assualt	Midway Home Entertainment	Teen (13+)	Animated Violence
Asteroids	Activision	Everyone	Mild Animated Violence
Atari Arcade's Greatest Hits	Atari Games/Williams	Kids To Adults	Mild Animated Violence
ATV Quad Power Racing	Acclaim	Everyone	No Descriptors
Auto Destruct	Electronic Arts	Teen (13+)	Animated Blood & Gore, Animated Violence
Azure Dreams	Konami USA, Inc.	Everyone	Mild Animated Violence, Mild Language
Backstreet Billiards	ASCII	Everyone	No Descriptors
Backyard Football	Humongous Entertainment	Everyone	No Descriptors
Ball Blazer Champions	Lucasarts	Kids To Adults	No Descriptors
Ball Breakers	Rockstar Games	Everyone	Animated Violence
Ballistic	Infogrames	Everyone	No Descriptors
Barbie Race and Ride PSX	Mattel Media INC.	Everyone	No Descriptors
Barbie Super Sports	Mattel Media INC.	Everyone	No Descriptors
Baseball 2000	Interplay Prods.	Everyone	No Descriptors
Bass Landing	AGETEC,Inc.	Everyone	No Descriptors
Bass Masters Classic Tournament Edition	THQ Inc.	Everyone	No Descriptors
Bass Rise	Bandai America	Everyone	No Descriptors
Batman and Robin	Acclaim	Teen (13+)	Animated Violence
Batman Forever The Arcade Game	Acclaim	Kids To Adults	Animated Violence
Battle Arena Toshinden 3	Playmates	Teen (13+)	Animated Violence
Battle Sport	Acclaim	Kids To Adults	Animated Violence
Battle Tank Global Assault	3 DO	Teen (13+)	Animated Violence
Battleship PSX	Hasbro Interactive	Everyone	Animated Violence
BattleStations	Electronic Arts	Kids To Adults	Animated Violence
Beast Wars Transformers	Hasbro Interactive	Kids To Adults	Animated Violence
Beast Wars Transmetals PSX	Bay Area Multimedia	Teen (13+)	Animated Violence
Beavis and Butthead Get Big	GT Interactive	Teen (13+)	Comic Mischief, Mild Language, Suggestive Themes
Bedlam	GT Interactive	Teen (13+)	Animated Violence, Animated Blood
Beyond the Beyond	Sony Interactive - Foster City	Kids To Adults	Animated Violence
Big Air	Accolade, Inc.	Everyone	No Descriptors
Big Bass World Championship with Hank Parker	Hot B USA	Kids To Adults	No Descriptors
Big ol Bass Fishermans Bait 2	Konami USA, Inc.	Everyone	No Descriptors
Bio F R E A K S	Midway Home Entertainment	Mature (17+)	Animated Blood & Gore, Animated Violence
Black Bass With Blue Marlin Featuring Hank Parker	Hot B USA	Everyone	No Descriptors
Black Dawn	Virgin Interactive	Teen (13+)	Animated Violence
Blast Chamber	Activision	Teen (13+)	Animated Violence
Blast Radius	Psygnosis	Everyone	Animated Violence
Blaster Master Blasting Again	Sunsoft	Everyone	Animated Violence
Blasto	Sony Computer Entertainment	Teen (13+)	Animated Violence, Mild Language, Suggestive Themes
Blitz 2000	Midway Home Entertainment	Teen (13+)	Animated Violence, Mild Language
Blitz 2001	Midway Home Entertainment	Everyone	Animated Violence
Bloody Roar	Sony Computer Entertainment	Teen (13+)	Animated Blood, Animated Violence
Bloody Roar 2	989 Studios	Teen (13+)	Animated Blood, Animated Violence, Suggestive Themes
Blue's Big Musical	Mattel Media INC.	Early Childhood	No Descriptors
Bomberman Fantasy Race	Atlus Software	Everyone	Mild Animated Violence
Bomberman World	Atlus Software	Everyone	Animated Violence
Boombots	Southpeak Interactive	Teen (13+)	Animated Violence, Comic Mischief
Brahma Force The Assault on Beltlogger 9	Jaleco	Kids To Adults	Animated Violence
Brave Fencer Musashi	Square Electronics	Everyone	Animated Violence
Bravo Air Race	THQ Inc.	Kids To Adults	No Descriptors
Breakout	Hasbro Interactive	Everyone	No Descriptors
Breakpoint Tennis	Acclaim	Kids To Adults	No Descriptors
Breath of Fire III	CAPCOM	Teen (13+)	Mild Animated Violence, Suggestive Themes
Brigandine	Atlus Software	Everyone	Animated Violence, Mild Language
Broken Helix	Konami USA, Inc.	Mature (17+)	Animated Blood, Animated Violence

Broken Sword	THQ Inc.	Teen (13+)	Animated Violence, Mild Language
Broken Sword II The Smoking Mirror	Crave Entertainment	Teen (13+)	Animated Blood, Animated Violence, Mild Language
Brunswick Circuit Pro Bowling	THQ Inc.	Everyone	No Descriptors
Brunswick Circuit Pro Bowling 2	Acclaim	Kids To Adults	No Descriptors
Bubble Bobble	Accolade, Inc.	Kids To Adults	No Descriptors
Bubsy 3D	GT Interactive	Kids To Adults	Animated Violence
Bugriders	Jaleco	Everyone	No Descriptors
Builders Block	Playmates	Kids To Adults	No Descriptors
Burning Road	Sony Computer Entertainment	Teen (13+)	Animated Blood, Animated Violence
Bushido Blade	Square Electronics	Teen (13+)	Animated Blood, Animated Violence
Bushido Blade 2	989 Studios	Everyone	Mild Language
Bust A Groove	Enix America Inc.	Everyone	Comic Mischief
Bust A Groove 2	Acclaim	Everyone	No Descriptors
Bust a Move 3DX	Natsume Inc.	Everyone	No Descriptors
Bust A Move 4	Activision	Everyone	Animated Violence
Buzz Lightyear of Star Command	Konami USA, Inc.	Teen (13+)	Animated Violence, Mild Language
C The Contra Adventure	Interplay Prods.	Kids To Adults	Gaming
Caesars Palace	Interplay Prods.	Everyone	Gaming
Caesars Palace 2	Interplay Prods.	Everyone	Gaming
Caesars Palace 2000	Activision	Kids To Adults	No Descriptors
Car and Driver Presents Grand Tour Racing	Sony Interactive - Foster City	Mature (17+)	Animated Blood & Gore, Animated Violence
Cardinal Syn	Interplay Prods.	Mature (17+)	Animated Blood & Gore, Animated Violence
Carmageddon	Sony Interactive - Foster City	Kids To Adults	Animated Violence
Carnage Heart	Sony Interactive - San Diego	Kids To Adults	No Descriptors
Cart World Series	Konami USA, Inc.	Teen (13+)	Animated Blood & Gore, Animated Violence
Castlevania Symphony of the Night	Electronic Arts	Everyone	Animated Violence
Castrol Honda Superbike World Champions	Hasbro Interactive	Everyone	Comic Mischief
Catdog Saving Mean Bob	Hasbro Interactive	Everyone	Mild Animated Violence
Centipede	Hasbro Interactive	Everyone	Mild Animated Violence
Centipede	Electronic Arts	Everyone	No Descriptors
Championship Bass	THQ Inc.	Everyone	No Descriptors
Championship Motocross 2001 Featuring Ricky Carmichael	THQ Inc.	Everyone	No Descriptors
Championship Motocross featuring Ricky Carmichael	Acclaim	Kids To Adults	Animated Violence
Cheesy	Square Electronics	Everyone	Mild Animated Violence
Chocobo Racing	SQUARE SOFT, Inc.	Everyone	Mild Animated Violence
Chocobo's Dungeon 2	Square Electronics	Teen (13+)	Animated Violence, Mild Language
Chrono Cross	Mindscape	Everyone	No Descriptors
Circuit Breakers	Psygnosis	Teen (13+)	Animated Violence
City of Lost Children	Activision	Everyone	Mild Animated Violence
Civilization 2	Interplay Prods.	Teen (13+)	Comic Mischief, Mild Animated Violence
Clayfighter 63 1 3 And Clayfighter Extreme	ASCII	Mature (17+)	Animated Blood & Gore, Animated Violence
Clock Tower	ASCII	Mature (17+)	Animated Blood & Gore, Animated Violence
Clock Tower 2 The Struggle Within	Psygnosis	Mature (17+)	Animated Violence
Code name Tenka	989 Studios	Everyone	No Descriptors
Colin McRae Rally Racing	Psygnosis	Kids To Adults	Animated Violence
Colony Wars	Psygnosis - US	Everyone	Animated Violence
Colony Wars Red Sun	Psygnosis	Everyone	Animated Violence
Colony Wars Vengeance	Westwood Studios, Inc.	Teen (13+)	Animated Violence, Use of Tobacco & Alcohol
Command and Conquer Red Alert Retaliation	Westwood Studios, Inc.	Teen (13+)	Realistic Violence
Command Conquer Red Alert	989 Studios	Everyone	Animated Violence
Contender	Konami USA, Inc.	Teen (13+)	Animated Violence
Contra Legacy of War	Sony Interactive - Foster City	Kids To Adults	No Descriptors
Cool Boarders	Sony Computer Entertainment	Kids To Adults	No Descriptors
Cool Boarders 2	989 Studios	Everyone	No Descriptors
Cool Boarders 3	989 Studios	Everyone	No Descriptors
Cool Boarders 4	Bandai America	Mature (17+)	Animated Blood & Gore, Animated Violence
Countdown Vampires	GT Interactive	Kids To Adults	Animated Violence
Courier Crisis	Activision	Mature (17+)	Animated Blood & Gore, Animated Violence
Covert Ops Nuclear Dawn	Sony Interactive - Foster City	Kids To Adults	No Descriptors
Crash Bandicoot	Sony Computer Entertainment	Kids To Adults	No Descriptors
Crash Bandicoot 2	989 Studios	Everyone	Mild Animated Violence
Crash Bandicoot 3 Warped	989 Studios	Everyone	Mild Animated Violence
Crash Team Racing	Interplay Prods.	Teen (13+)	Animated Violence
Crime Killers	Single Trac	Teen (13+)	Animated Blood, Animated Violence
Critical Depth	Fox Interactive	Kids To Adults	Mild Animated Violence
Croc	Fox Interactive	Everyone	Mild Animated Violence
Croc 2	Acclaim	Mature (17+)	Animated Violence, Animated Blood
Crow City of Angels	Origin Systems	Mature (17+)	Animated Violence
Crusader No Remorse Playstation and Saturn	3 DO	Teen (13+)	Animated Blood, Animated Violence
Crusaders of Might and Magic	Konami USA, Inc.	Teen (13+)	Animated Violence, Animated Blood & Gore
Crypt Killer	Electronic Arts	Everyone	No Descriptors
Cyber Tiger	THQ Inc.	Teen (13+)	Animated Blood, Animated Violence, Suggestive Themes
Danger Girl	Mindscape	Kids To Adults	No Descriptors
Dare Devil Derby 3D	Fujitsu	Everyone	Animated Violence
Darius Gaiden	Electronic Arts	Kids To Adults	Animated Violence
Darklight Conflict	CAPCOM	Teen (13+)	Animated Blood, Animated Violence
Darkstalkers 3	Gathering of Developers	Teen (13+)	Animated Blood & Gore, Animated Violence
Darkstone	Acclaim	Everyone	Mild Language
Dave Mirra Freestyle BMX	GT Interactive	Teen (13+)	Animated Blood, Animated Violence
Dead Ball Zone	ASC American Softworks	Everyone	Animated Violence
Dead in the Water	Tecmo	Teen (13+)	Animated Violence, Suggestive Themes
Dead or Alive	Eidos Interactive (formerly US GOLD)	Mature (17+)	Animated Blood & Gore, Animated Violence
Deathtrap Dungeon	Tecmo	Mature (17+)	Animated Blood, Animated Violence
Deception III " Dark Delusion¹	Interplay Prods.	Teen (13+)	Animated Violence
Descent Maximum	KOEI Corp.	Teen (13+)	Animated Violence, Mild Language
Destrega	Psygnosis	Kids To Adults	No Descriptors
Destruction Derby 2	Midway Home Entertainment	Everyone	No Descriptors
Destruction Derby Raw	THQ Inc.	Everyone	No Descriptors
Devil Dice	Electronic Arts	Mature (17+)	Animated Blood & Gore, Animated Violence
Diablo	Fox Interactive	Mature (17+)	Animated Blood & Gore, Animated Violence
Die Hard Trilogy 2	Bandai America	Teen (13+)	Comic Mischief
Digimon World	CAPCOM	Mature (17+)	Animated Blood & Gore, Animated Violence
Dino Crisis	CAPCOM	Mature (17+)	Animated Blood & Gore, Animated Violence
Dino Crisis 2	Ubi Soft	Everyone	Animated Violence
Disney's Dinosaur	Ubi Soft	Everyone	Mild Animated Violence
Disney's Donald Duck Goin Quackers	NewKidCo	Everyone	No Descriptors
Disney's Story Studio Mulan	Universal Interactive Studios, Inc.	Teen (13+)	Animated Violence
Disruptor	Namco Hometek	Teen (13+)	Animated Violence
Dragon Valor	Bandai America	Teen (13+)	Animated Violence
DragonBall GT	Acclaim	Teen (13+)	Animated Violence, Animated Blood
DragonHeart Fire and Steel	Jaleco	Teen (13+)	Animated Blood, Animated Violence
Dragonseeds	Cryo Interactive Entertainment	Teen (13+)	Animated Violence
Dreams to Reality	GT Interactive	Teen (13+)	Mild Language
Driver	GT Interactive	Mature (17+)	Animated Blood & Gore, Animated Violence, Strong Sexual Content
Duke Nukem land of the Babes	GT Interactive	Mature (17+)	Animated Blood & Gore, Animated Violence, Strong Sexual Content
Duke Nukem Time to Kill	GT Interactive	Mature (17+)	Animated Blood & Gore, Animated Violence, Strong Sexual Content
Duke Nukem Total Meltdown PSX	Southpeak Interactive	Everyone	Mild Animated Violence, Use of Tobacco & Alcohol
Dukes of Hazzard	Westwood Studios, Inc.	Teen (13+)	Animated Blood, Realistic Violence
Dune 2000	KOEI Corp.	Teen (13+)	Animated Blood & Gore, Animated Violence
Dynasty Warriors	Electronic Arts	Everyone	No Descriptors
EA Sports Supercross 2000	Infogrames	Everyone	Animated Violence
Eagle One Harrier Attack	ASCII	Teen (13+)	Animated Blood, Mild Language
Echo Night	Acclaim	Teen (13+)	Animated Blood, Mature Sexual Themes, Strong Language
ECW Anarchy Rulz	Acclaim	Mature (17+)	Animated Violence, Strong Language
ECW Hardcore Revolution			

Eggs of Steel	Atlus Software	Everyone	Comic Mischief
Ehrgeiz	SQUARE SOFT, Inc.	Teen (13+)	Animated Violence
Einhander	Sony Computer Entertainment	Everyone	Animated Violence
Elemental Gearbolt	Working Design	Teen (13+)	Animated Violence
Eliminator	Psygnosis - US	Everyone	Animated Violence
Elmo's Letter Adventure	NewKidCo	Early Childhood	Edutainment
Elmo's Number Journey	NewKidCo	Early Childhood	Edutainment
Epidemic	Sony Interactive - Foster City	Kids To Adults	Animated Violence
ESPN Digital Games NBA Tonight 99	Radical Entertainment	Everyone	No Descriptors
ESPN Digital Pro Boarders	Radical Entertainment	Everyone	No Descriptors
ESPN Great Outdoor Games Bass Fishing	Konami USA, Inc.	Everyone	No Descriptors
Eternal Eyes	Sunsoft	Everyone	Animated Violence
Evil Zone	Titus Software - CALIF	Teen (13+)	Animated Violence, Suggestive Themes
Excalibur 2555 A D	Sir Tech Software	Teen (13+)	Animated Blood, Animated Violence
Expendable	Infogrames	Teen (13+)	Animated Blood & Gore, Animated Violence
F1 2000	Electronic Arts	Everyone	No Descriptors
F1 Championship	Ubi Soft	Everyone	No Descriptors
F1 World Grand Prix	Eidos Interactive	Everyone	No Descriptors
Fallout	Interplay Prods.	Mature (17+)	Animated Blood & Gore
Family Game Pack Royale	3 DO	Everyone	No Descriptors
Fantastic Four	Acclaim	Kids To Adults	Animated Violence
Fatal Fury Wild Animation	SNK Corporation of America	Teen (13+)	Animated Violence
Fear Effect	Eidos Interactive	Mature (17+)	Animated Blood & Gore, Animated Violence, Suggestive Themes
Felony 11 79	ASCII	Kids To Adults	Animated Violence
FIFA 2000	Electronic Arts	Everyone	No Descriptors
FIFA 99	Electronic Arts	Everyone	No Descriptors
FIFA Soccer 97	Electronic Arts	Kids To Adults	No Descriptors
FIFA The Road to World Cup 98	Electronic Arts	Kids To Adults	No Descriptors
Fighting Force	Eidos Interactive (formerly US GOLD)	Teen (13+)	Animated Blood, Animated Violence
Fighting Force 2	Eidos Interactive	Teen (13+)	Animated Blood, Animated Violence
Final Doom	Williams Entertainment, Inc.	Mature (17+)	Animated Violence, Animated Blood & Gore
Final Fantasy Anthology	Square Electronics	Teen (13+)	Comic Mischief, Mild Animated Violence
Final Fantasy Tactics	Sony Computer Entertainment	Teen (13+)	Animated Violence, Mild Language
Final Fantasy VIII	SQUARE SOFT, Inc.	Teen (13+)	Animated Violence, Mild Language, Suggestive Themes
Final Fantasy VII	Sony Computer Entertainment	Teen (13+)	Comic Mischief, Mild Animated Violence, Mild Language
Final Fantasy VII Demo	Sony Interactive - Foster City	Teen (13+)	Animated Violence
Fisherman's Bait	Konami USA, Inc.	Everyone	No Descriptors
Flintstones Bowling	Southpeak Interactive	Everyone	No Descriptors
Formula 1 97	Psygnosis	Kids To Adults	No Descriptors
Formula 1 98	Psygnosis - US	Everyone	No Descriptors
Formula One	Psygnosis	Everyone	No Descriptors
Forsaken	Acclaim	Mature (17+)	Animated Blood & Gore, Animated Violence
Fox Sports Interactive Golf 99	Fox Interactive	Everyone	No Descriptors
Fox Sports Interactive Soccer 99	Fox Interactive	Everyone	No Descriptors
Freestyle Boardin 99	CAPCOM	Freestyle	No Descriptors
Frogger 2	Hasbro Interactive	Everyone	No Descriptors
Frogger 3D	Hasbro Interactive	Kids To Adults	No Descriptors
Front Mission 3	Square Electronics	Teen (13+)	Animated Violence
Future Cop L A P D	Electronic Arts	Teen (13+)	Animated Blood, Animated Violence
G Darius	THQ Inc.	Everyone	Animated Violence
G Police	Psygnosis	Kids To Adults	Animated Violence
G Police Weapons of Justice	Psygnosis - US	Teen (13+)	Animated Violence
Galaga	Hasbro Interactive	Everyone	Mild Animated Violence
Galerians	Crave Entertainment	Mature (17+)	Animated Blood & Gore, Animated Violence
Gallop Racer	Tecmo	Everyone	No Descriptors
Game of Life	Hasbro Interactive	Everyone	No Descriptors
Gameday 2001	Sony Computer Entertainment America	Everyone	No Descriptors
Gauntlet Legends	Atari Games/Williams	Teen (13+)	Animated Blood, Animated Violence
Gekido	Interplay Prods.	Teen (13+)	Animated Blood, Animated Violence
Gex 3 Deep Cover Gecko	Crystal Dynamics	Teen (13+)	Comic Mischief, Suggestive Themes
Gex Enter The Gecko	Crystal Dynamics	Kids To Adults	Animated Violence, Comic Mischief, Mild Language
Ghost in the Shell	THQ Inc.	Teen (13+)	Animated Violence
Global Domination	Psygnosis - US	Everyone	Animated Violence
Glover	Hasbro Interactive	Everyone	Comic Mischief
Goal Storm 97	Konami USA, Inc.	Kids To Adults	No Descriptors
Golf	Sony Computer Entertainment	Kids To Adults	No Descriptors
Gran Turismo	Sony Computer Entertainment	Everyone	No Descriptors
Grand Slam 97	Virgin Interactive	Kids To Adults	No Descriptors
Grand Theft Auto	Take 2 Interactive Software, Inc.	Mature (17+)	Animated Blood, Strong Language
Grand Theft Auto 2	Take 2 Interactive Software, Inc.	Teen (13+)	Animated Violence, Strong Language, Suggestive Themes
Grand Theft Auto Add ON	Take 2 Interactive Software, Inc.	Mature (17+)	Animated Blood, Strong Language
Grand Turismo 2	989 Studios	Everyone	No Descriptors
Grandia	989 Studios	Everyone	Comic Mischief, Mild Animated Violence
Grid Runner	Virgin Interactive	Kids To Adults	Animated Violence
Grind Session	Sony Computer Entertainment America	Everyone	Mild Animated Violence
Grudge Warriors	Take 2 Interactive Software, Inc.	Teen (13+)	Animated Violence
Guardian Legends	Activision	Everyone	Mild Animated Violence
Guilty Gear	Atlus Software	Teen (13+)	Animated Blood, Animated Violence
Hardball 6	Accolade, Inc.	Everyone	No Descriptors
Heart of Darkness	Interplay Prods.	Everyone	Animated Violence, Use of Tobacco & Alcohol
Hello Kitty's Cube Frenzy	NewKidCo	Everyone	No Descriptors
Herc's Adventures	Lucasarts	Kids To Adults	Mild Animated Violence, Comic Mischief
Hercules	Virgin Interactive	Kids To Adults	Animated Violence
Hexen	GT Interactive	Mature (17+)	Animated Violence, Animated Blood
High Heat Baseball 2001	3 DO	Everyone	No Descriptors
Hogs of War	Infogrames	Teen (13+)	Animated Blood, Comic Mischief, Mild Language
Hot Shots Golf 2	Sony Computer Entertainment America	Everyone	No Descriptors
Hot Wheels RPM Racing	Electronic Arts	Everyone	Mild Animated Violence
Hydro Thunder Racing Association	Midway Home Entertainment	Everyone	Mild Animated Violence
Hyperblade	Activision	Teen (13+)	Animated Violence, Animated Blood & Gore
I Q Intelligent Cube	Sony Computer Entertainment	Kids To Adults	No Descriptors
ID4	Fox Interactive	Kids To Adults	Animated Violence
Impact Racing	Acclaim	Kids To Adults	Animated Violence
In Cold Blood	Midway Home Entertainment	Teen (13+)	Animated Blood, Animated Violence
In the Zone 2000	Konami USA, Inc.	Everyone	No Descriptors
Incredible Crises	Interplay Prods.	Teen (13+)	Animated Violence, Comic Mischief, Suggestive Themes
Intellivision Classics	Activision	Everyone	No Descriptors
International Superstar Soccer 98	Konami USA, Inc.	Everyone	No Descriptors
International Track and Field 2000	Konami USA, Inc.	Everyone	No Descriptors
Invasion From Beyond	GT Interactive	Everyone	Animated Violence
Iron Blood	Acclaim	Teen (13+)	Animated Violence, Animated Blood
Iron Soldier 3	Vatical Entertainment	Teen (13+)	Animated Violence
IronMan X O	Acclaim	Teen (13+)	Animated Violence
Irritating Stick	Jaleco	Everyone	No Descriptors
ISS Pro Evolution	Konami USA, Inc.	Everyone	No Descriptors
Jackie Chan's Stuntmaster	Midway Home Entertainment	Teen (13+)	Animated Violence
Jade Cocoon Story of the Tamamayu	Crave Entertainment	Teen (13+)	Mild Animated Violence, Mild Language
James Bond Tomorrow Never Dies	Electronic Arts	Teen (13+)	Animated Blood, Animated Violence, Suggestive Themes
Jeff Gordon XS Racing	ASC American Softworks	Everyone	No Descriptors
Jeopardy	Hasbro Interactive	Everyone	No Descriptors
Jeremy McGrath SuperCross 2000	Acclaim	Everyone	No Descriptors
Jeremy McGrath's Super Cross 98	Acclaim	Everyone, Kids To Adults	No Descriptors
Jersey Devil	Sony Interactive - Foster City	Everyone	Comic Mischief
Jet Moto	Sony Interactive - Foster City	Kids To Adults	No Descriptors

Title	Publisher	Rating	Descriptors
Jet Moto 2	Sony Computer Entertainment	Kids To Adults	No Descriptors
Jet Moto 2 Ltd Edition	989 Studios	Everyone	No Descriptors
Jet Moto 3	989 Studios	Everyone	No Descriptors
Jimmy Johnson's VR Football 98	Interplay Prods.	Kids To Adults	No Descriptors
JoJo's Bizzarre Adventure	CAPCOM	Teen (13+)	Animated Violence, Suggestive Themes
Judge Dredd	Activision	Teen (13+)	Animated Violence
Juggernaut	Jaleco	Mature (17+)	Animated Blood & Gore
Jumping Flash 2	Sony Interactive - Foster City	Kids To Adults	Mild Animated Violence
K 1 Grand Prix	Jaleco	Everyone	Animated Violence, Realistic Violence
K 1 Revenge	Jaleco	Everyone	Animated Violence, Realistic Violence
K1 The Arena Fighters	THQ Inc.	Kids To Adults	Animated Violence
Kagero Deception II	Tecmo	Mature (17+)	Animated Blood, Animated Violence
Kartia	Atlus Software	Everyone	Animated Violence, Mild Language
Kensei Sacred First	Konami USA, Inc.	Teen (13+)	Animated Violence
Killer Loop	Crave Entertainment	Everyone	Mild Animated Violence
Killing Zone	Acclaim	Teen (13+)	Animated Violence, Animated Blood
King of Fighters Evolution	SNK Corporation of America	Teen (13+)	Animated Violence, Suggestive Themes
King's Field II	ASCII	Teen (13+)	Animated Violence
Kingdom II Shadoan	TIG Publishing	Kids To Adults	Animated Violence
Kingsley	Psygnosis - US	Everyone	Animated Violence
Klonoa	Namco Hometek	Everyone	No Descriptors
Knockout Kings	Electronic Arts	Everyone	Animated Blood, Animated Violence
Knockout Kings 2000	Electronic Arts	Teen (13+)	Animated Violence
Konami Arcade Classics	Konami USA, Inc.	Everyone	Animated Violence
Koudelka	Infogrames	Mature (17+)	Animated Blood & Gore, Animated Violence
Kula World	Psygnosis - US	Everyone	No Descriptors
Kurt Warner's Arena Football Unleashed	Midway Home Entertainment	Teen (13+)	Mild Animated Violence
Legacy of Kain Soul Reaver	Crystal Dynamics	Mature (17+)	Animated Blood, Animated Violence
Legend of Dragoon	989 Studios	Teen (13+)	Animated Blood, Animated Violence
Legend of Legaia	Sony Interactive - Foster City	Everyone	Animated Violence
Legend of Mana	Square Electronics	Teen (13+)	Mild Animated Violence, Suggestive Themes
Lego Racers	Lego Media	Everyone	No Descriptors
Lego Rock Raiders	Lego Media	Everyone	No Descriptors
Lethal Enforcers 1 2	Konami USA, Inc.	Mature (17+)	Realistic Violence
Lode Runner	Natsume Inc.	Kids To Adults	Animated Violence
Logical	Conspiracy Entertainment Corporation	Everyone	No Descriptors
Looney Tunes Racing	Infogrames	Everyone	Comic Mischief
Lucky Luke	Ocean of America	Everyone	Animated Violence
Lunar 2 Eternal Blue Complete Demo	Working Design	Teen (13+)	Mild Animated Violence, Mild Language, Suggestive Themes
Lunar 2 Trailer	Working Design	Everyone	Suitable for All Users
Lunar Silver Star Story Complete	Working Design	Teen (13+)	Animated Violence, Suggestive Themes
Mace the Dark Age	Atari Games/Williams	Mature (17+)	Animated Blood, Animated Violence
Machine Hunter	MGM Interactive	Teen (13+)	Animated Blood & Gore, Animated Violence
Madden NFL 2001	Electronic Arts	Everyone	No Descriptors
Madden NFL 97	Electronic Arts	Kids To Adults	No Descriptors
Madden NFL 98	Electronic Arts	Kids To Adults	No Descriptors
Madden NFL 99	Electronic Arts	Everyone	No Descriptors
MAG 3	Crave Entertainment	Everyone	Mild Animated Violence
Magic The Gathering Battle Mage	Acclaim	Teen (13+)	Animated Violence
Magical Tetris Challenge Featuring Mickey	CAPCOM	Everyone	No Descriptors
Major League Baseball 2001	Fox Interactive	Everyone	No Descriptors
March Madness 2000	Electronic Arts	Everyone	No Descriptors
March Madness 98	Electronic Arts	Kids To Adults	No Descriptors
March Madness 99	Electronic Arts	Everyone	No Descriptors
Martian Gothic	Rockstar Games	Mature (17+)	Animated Blood & Gore, Animated Violence
Marvel Super Heroes	CAPCOM	Teen (13+)	Animated Violence
Marvel Super Heroes Vs Street Fighter	CAPCOM	Teen (13+)	Animated Violence
Marvel vs Capcom	CAPCOM	Teen (13+)	Animated Violence
Masic The Gathering Battle Mase	Acclaim	Teen (13+)	Animated Violence
Mass Destruction	BMG Interactive	Teen (13+)	Animated Violence
Mass Destruction	ASC American Softworks	Teen (13+)	Animated Violence
Master of Monsters	ASCII	Everyone	Animated Blood, Animated Violence
Maximum Force	Midway Home Entertainment	Mature (17+)	Animated Blood, Animated Violence
MDK	Playmates	Teen (13+)	Animated Blood, Animated Violence
Medal of Honor	Electronic Arts	Teen (13+)	Animated Violence
Medi Evil	989 Studios	Teen (13+)	Animated Blood, Animated Violence
Medi Evil 2	Sony Computer Entertainment America	Teen (13+)	Animated Blood, Animated Violence
Mega Man 8	CAPCOM	Kids To Adults	Animated Violence
Mega Man Battle and Chase	CAPCOM	Kids To Adults	No Descriptors
Mega Man Legends	CAPCOM	Everyone	Animated Violence
Mega Man X4	CAPCOM	Kids To Adults	Animated Blood, Animated Violence
Metal Gear Solid	Konami USA, Inc.	Mature (17+)	Animated Blood & Gore, Animated Violence, Mature Sexual Themes
Metal Gear Solid VR Missions	Konami USA, Inc.	Mature (17+)	Animated Blood, Animated Violence
Micro Machines	Midway Home Entertainment	Kids To Adults	Mild Animated Violence
Micro Machines V3	CODEMASTERS SOFTWARE LIMITED	Everyone	Mild Animated Violence
Micro Maniacs	Codemasters	Everyone	Animated Blood, Animated Violence
Midway Presents Arcades Greatest Hits Midway Collection II	Midway Home Entertainment	Kids To Adults	Mild Animated Violence
Mike Tyson's Boxing	Codemasters	Teen (13+)	Animated Violence
Miss Spider's Tea Party	Simon & Schuster Interactive	Early Childhood	Edutainment
Missile Command	Hasbro Interactive	Everyone	Animated Violence
Mission Impossible	Ocean of America	Teen (13+)	Animated Violence
MLB 2000	Sony Interactive - Foster City	Everyone	No Descriptors
MLB 2001	Sony Computer Entertainment America	Everyone	No Descriptors
MLB 98	Sony Computer Entertainment	Kids To Adults	No Descriptors
MLB 99	Sony Computer Entertainment	Everyone, Kids To Adults	No Descriptors
MLBPA Bottom Of The 9th 97	Konami USA, Inc.	Kids To Adults	No Descriptors
MLBPA Bottom Of The Ninth	Konami USA, Inc.	Everyone	No Descriptors
MLS Gamenight	Konami USA, Inc.	Everyone	No Descriptors
Monaco Grand Prix	Ubi Soft	Everyone	No Descriptors
Monkey Hero	Take 2 Interactive Software, Inc.	Everyone	No Descriptors
Monkey Magic	Sunsoft	Everyone	Animated Violence
Monster Rancher	Tecmo	Kids To Adults	Animated Violence
Monster Rancher 2	Tecmo	Everyone	Animated Violence
Monster Rancher Battle Card	Tecmo	Everyone	Mild Animated Violence
Monster Seed	Sunsoft	Everyone	Animated Violence
Mort the Chicken	Crave Entertainment	Everyone	No Descriptors
Mortal Kombat 4	Midway Home Entertainment	Mature (17+)	Animated Blood & Gore, Animated Violence
Mortal Kombat Mortal Kombat II	Acclaim	Mature (17+)	Realistic Violence, Realistic Blood & Gore
Mortal Kombat Mythologies	Midway Home Entertainment	Mature (17+)	Animated Blood & Gore, Animated Violence
Mortal Kombat Special Forces	Midway Home Entertainment	Mature (17+)	Animated Blood, Animated Violence
Mortal Kombat Trilogy	Williams Entertainment, Inc.	Mature (17+)	Realistic Violence, Realistic Blood & Gore
Moto Racer	Electronic Arts	Kids To Adults	No Descriptors
Moto Racer 2	Electronic Arts	Everyone	No Descriptors
Motor Toon Grand Prix	Sony Interactive - Foster City	Kids To Adults	No Descriptors
Motorhead	Fox Sports Interactive	Everyone	No Descriptors
Mr Driller	Namco Hometek	Everyone	No Descriptors
Ms PacMan Maze Madness	Namco Hometek	Everyone	No Descriptors
MTV Sports Pure Ride	THQ Inc.	Everyone	No Descriptors
MTV Sports Skateboarding Featuring Andy Macdonald	THQ Inc.	Everyone	Mild Animated Violence, Mild Language
MTV Sports Snowboarding	THQ Inc.	Everyone	Mild Language
Muppet Monster Adventure	Midway Home Entertainment	Everyone	Mild Animated Violence
Muppet Race Mania	Midway Home Entertainment	Everyone	Comic Mischief
Music 2K Music 2000 MTV Jam	CODEMASTERS SOFTWARE LIMITED	Everyone	No Descriptors
N20 Nitrous Oxide	Fox Interactive	Teen (13+)	Animated Violence
Nagano Winter Olympics 98	Konami USA, Inc.	Kids To Adults	No Descriptors
Namco Museum Vol 3	Namco Hometek	Kids To Adults	Mild Animated Violence, Comic Mischief
Namco Museum Vol 4	Namco Hometek	Kids To Adults	Animated Violence

Namco Museum Vol 5	Namco Hometek	Kids To Adults	Animated Violence
NanoTek Warrior	Virgin Interactive	Kids To Adults	Animated Violence
Nascar 2000	Electronic Arts	Everyone	No Descriptors
NASCAR 2001	Electronic Arts	Everyone	No Descriptors
Nascar 98	Electronic Arts	Kids To Adults	No Descriptors
NASCAR 98 50th Anniversary Edition	Electronic Arts	Everyone, Kids To Adults	No Descriptors
NASCAR 99	Electronic Arts	Everyone	No Descriptors
NASCAR Heat	Hasbro Interactive	Everyone	No Descriptors
Nascar Legacy	Electronic Arts	Everyone	No Descriptors
Nascar Racing	Sierra On-Line	Kids To Adults	No Descriptors
Nascar Rumble	Electronic Arts	Everyone	No Descriptors
NBA Championship 2000	Fox Interactive	Everyone	No Descriptors
NBA Fastbreak	Midway Home Entertainment	Kids To Adults	No Descriptors
NBA HangTime	Williams Entertainment, Inc.	Kids To Adults	No Descriptors
NBA In The Zone 2	Konami USA, Inc.	Kids To Adults	No Descriptors
NBA In the Zone 98	Konami USA, Inc.	Kids To Adults	No Descriptors
NBA in the Zone 99	Konami USA, Inc.	Everyone	No Descriptors
NBA JAM Extreme	Acclaim	Kids To Adults	No Descriptors
NBA Live 2000	Electronic Arts	Everyone	No Descriptors
NBA Live 97	Electronic Arts	Kids To Adults	No Descriptors
NBA LIVE 98	Electronic Arts	Kids To Adults	No Descriptors
NBA Live 99	Electronic Arts	Everyone	No Descriptors
NBA Shootout2000	989 Studios	Everyone	No Descriptors
NBA Shootout 97	Sony Interactive - Foster City	Kids To Adults	No Descriptors
NBA SHOOTOUT 98	Sony Computer Entertainment	Everyone	No Descriptors
NBA Showtime The NBA on NBC	Midway Home Entertainment	Everyone	No Descriptors
NCAA FINAL FOUR 2000	989 Studios	Everyone	No Descriptors
NCAA Final Four 99	989 Studios	Everyone	No Descriptors
NCAA Football 2000	Electronic Arts	Everyone	No Descriptors
NCAA Football 2001	Electronic Arts	Everyone	No Descriptors
NCAA Football98	Electronic Arts	Kids To Adults	No Descriptors
NCAA Football 99	Electronic Arts	Everyone	No Descriptors
NCAA Game Breaker	Sony Interactive - Foster City	Kids To Adults	No Descriptors
NCAA Game Breaker 98	Sony Interactive - Foster City	Kids To Adults	No Descriptors
NCAA Gamebreaker 2000	989 Studios	Everyone	No Descriptors
NCAA Gamebreaker 99	989 Studios	Everyone	No Descriptors
NecroDome	S.S.I.	Mature (17+)	Animated Blood & Gore, Animated Violence
Nectaris Military Madness	Jaleco	Teen (13+)	Animated Violence
Need for Speed High Stakes	Electronic Arts	Everyone	No Descriptors
Need for Speed Porshe Unleashed	Electronic Arts	Everyone	Informational
Newman Haas Racing	Psygnosis - US	Everyone	No Descriptors
NFL BLITZ	Midway Home Entertainment	Everyone	Animated Violence, Mild Language
NFL Extreme 2	989 Studios	Everyone	Animated Violence
NFL Gameday99	989 Studios	Everyone	No Descriptors
NFL Gameday 2000	989 Studios	Everyone	No Descriptors
NFL Gameday 97	Sony Interactive - Foster City	Kids To Adults	No Descriptors
NFL Gameday 98	Sony Interactive - Foster City	Kids To Adults	No Descriptors
NFL Quarterback Club 97	Acclaim	Kids To Adults	No Descriptors
NFL Xtreme	Sony Computer Entertainment	Everyone	Animated Violence, Mild Language
Ngen Racing	Infogrames	Everyone	Animated Violence
NHL 2000	Electronic Arts	Everyone	Animated Violence
NHL 97	Electronic Arts	Kids To Adults	Animated Violence
NHL 98	Electronic Arts	Kids To Adults	Animated Violence
NHL 99	Electronic Arts	Everyone	Animated Violence
NHL Blades of Steel 2000	Konami USA, Inc.	Everyone	Animated Violence
NHL Blades of Steel 99	Konami USA, Inc.	Everyone	Animated Violence
NHL Breakaway 98	Acclaim	Kids To Adults	Animated Violence
NHL Championship 2000	Fox Interactive	Everyone	Animated Violence
NHL Faceoff 2000	989 Studios	Everyone	Animated Violence
NHL Faceoff 98	Sony Computer Entertainment	Kids To Adults	Animated Violence
NHL Faceoff 97	Sony Interactive - Foster City	Kids To Adults	Animated Violence
NHL FACEOFF 99	989 Studios	Everyone	Animated Violence
NHL National Hockey Night 99	Radical Entertainment	Everyone	Animated Violence
NHL Powerplay 98	Virgin Interactive	Kids To Adults	Animated Violence
Nicktoons Racing	Hasbro Interactive	Everyone	No Descriptors
Nightmare Creatures	Activision	Mature (17+)	Animated Blood & Gore, Animated Violence
Nightmare Creatures II	Konami USA, Inc.	Mature (17+)	Animated Blood & Gore, Animated Violence
Ninja Shadows of Darkness	Eidos Interactive	Teen (13+)	Animated Violence
No Fear Downhill Mountain Bike Racing	Codemasters	Everyone	No Descriptors
No One Can Stop Mr Domino	Acclaim	Everyone	No Descriptors
Norse By Norse West	Interplay Prods.	Kids To Adults	Mild Animated Violence, Comic Mischief
Nuclear Strike	Electronic Arts	Teen (13+)	Animated Violence, Realistic Violence
O D T	Psygnosis - US	Teen (13+)	Animated Blood, Animated Violence
OddWorld	GT Interactive	Teen (13+)	Animated Blood, Animated Violence
Oddworld Abe's Exoddus	GT Interactive	Teen (13+)	Animated Blood, Animated Violence, Comic Mischief
Ogre Battle	Atlus Software	Kids To Adults	Animated Violence
Omega Boost	989 Studios	Everyone	Animated Violence
One	ASC American Softworks	Teen (13+)	Animated Violence
Open Ice	Midway Home Entertainment	Kids To Adults	No Descriptors
Over blood	Electronic Arts	Teen (13+)	Animated Violence
Overboard	Psygnosis	Kids To Adults	Animated Violence
Pac Man world	Namco Hometek	Everyone	No Descriptors
Pandemonium	Crystal Dynamics	Kids To Adults	No Descriptors
Pandemonium 2	Crystal Dynamics	Kids To Adults	No Descriptors
Paperboy	Midway Home Entertainment	Everyone	Mild Animated Violence
Parappa	Sony Computer Entertainment	Kids To Adults	No Descriptors
Parasite Eve	Square Electronics	Mature (17+)	Animated Violence, Mature Sexual Themes
Parasite Eve 2	Square Electronics	Mature (17+)	Animated Blood & Gore, Animated Violence
Parasite Eve Demo	Square Electronics	Teen (13+)	Suitable for Mature Users
Peak Performance	Atlus Software	Kids To Adults	No Descriptors
Pegasus Prime	Acclaim	Kids To Adults	No Descriptors
Perfect Weapon	ASC American Softworks	Teen (13+)	Animated Violence
Peter Jacobsen's Golden Tee Golf	Wizard Works Group Inc.	Everyone	No Descriptors
PGA European Tour	Infogrames	Everyone	No Descriptors
PGA Tour 97	Electronic Arts	Kids To Adults	No Descriptors
PGA Tour Golf 98	Electronic Arts	Kids To Adults	No Descriptors
Pitfall 3d Beyond The Jungle	Activision	Teen (13+)	Animated Violence
Play with the Teletubbies	Havas Interactive	Early Childhood	Edutainment
Pocket Fighter	CAPCOM	Teen (13+)	Mild Animated Violence
Point Blank	Namco Hometek	Teen (13+)	Animated Violence
Point Blant 2	Namco Hometek	Teen (13+)	Animated Violence
Polaris SnoCross	Vatical Entertainment	Everyone	No Descriptors
Pong	Hasbro Interactive	Everyone	No Descriptors
Pool Hustler	Activision	Everyone	Gaming, Mild Language
Pool Shark	THQ Inc.	Everyone	No Descriptors
Populous The Begining	Origin Systems	Teen (13+)	Animated Violence
Porsche Challenge	Sony Computer Entertainment	Kids To Adults	No Descriptors
Power Move Pro Wrestling	Activision	Kids To Adults	Animated Violence, Animated Blood
Power Rangers Zeo Full Tilt Battle Pinball	Bandai America	Kids To Adults	No Descriptors
Power Soccer 2	Psygnosis	Kids To Adults	No Descriptors
Powerslave PSX Saturn	Playmates	Mature (17+)	Animated Violence, Animated Blood & Gore
Poy Poy	Konami USA, Inc.	Kids To Adults	Animated Violence
Pro 18 World Tour Golf	Psygnosis - US	Everyone	No Descriptors
Pro Pinball	Interplay Prods.	Kids To Adults	No Descriptors
Pro Pinball Rige Race Usa	Empire Interactive	Everyone	No Descriptors
Pro Pinball Time Shock	Empire Interactive	Kids To Adults	No Descriptors
Professional Underground League of Pain	Psygnosis	Kids To Adults	Animated Violence
Project X2	Acclaim	Kids To Adults	Animated Violence

ESRB Tables • www.esrb.org

Title	Publisher	Rating	Descriptors
Psybadet	Psygnosis - US	Everyone	Comic Mischief
Psychic Force	Acclaim	Teen (13+)	Animated Violence
Punky Skunk	Jaleco	Kids To Adults	No Descriptors
Q*bert	Hasbro Interactive	Everyone	No Descriptors
Quake II	Activision	Mature (17+)	Animated Blood & Gore, Animated Violence
R C Stunt Copter	Interplay Prods.	Everyone	Mild Animated Violence, Mild Language
R Types	ASCII	Everyone	Mild Animated Violence
R Types Delta	AGETEC,Inc.	Everyone	Mild Animated Violence
R4 Ridge Racer Type 4	Namco Hometek	Everyone	No Descriptors
Rage Racer	Namco Hometek	Kids To Adults	No Descriptors
Railroad Tycoon II	Gathering of Developers	Everyone	No Descriptors
Rally Cross 2	989 Studios	Everyone	No Descriptors
Rally Racing Championship	Electronic Arts	Everyone	No Descriptors
Rampage 2 Universal Tour	Midway Home Entertainment	Teen (13+)	Comic Mischief
Rampage Through Time	Midway Home Entertainment	Teen (13+)	Comic Mischief
Rampage World Tour	Midway Home Entertainment	Teen (13+)	Comic Mischief
Rascal	Psygnosis - US	Everyone	Mild Animated Violence
Rat Attack	Mindscape	Everyone	No Descriptors
Ray Tracers	THQ Inc.	Kids To Adults	No Descriptors
Raycrisis	Working Design	Everyone	Animated Violence
Raystorm	Working Design	Kids To Adults	Animated Violence
RC de Go	Acclaim	Everyone	No Descriptors
RC Revenge	Midway Home Entertainment	Everyone	Mild Animated Violence
Ready To Rumble Boxing	Midway Home Entertainment	Teen (13+)	Animated Violence
Real Bout Fatal Fury	Sony Computer Entertainment	Teen (13+)	Animated Violence, Animated Blood
ReBoot	Electronic Arts	Kids To Adults	Animated Violence
Red Asphalt	Interplay Prods.	Kids To Adults	Animated Violence
Reel Fishing	Natsume Inc.	Kids To Adults	No Descriptors
Reel Fishing II	Natsume Inc.	Everyone	No Descriptors
Reloaded	Interplay Prods.	Mature (17+)	Animated Violence, Animated Blood & Gore
Renegade Racers	Interplay Prods.	Everyone	Mild Animated Violence
Resident Evil 2	CAPCOM	Mature (17+)	Animated Blood & Gore, Animated Violence
Resident Evil 3 Nemesis	CAPCOM	Mature (17+)	Animated Blood & Gore, Animated Violence
Resident Evil Director S Cut	CAPCOM	Mature (17+)	Animated Blood & Gore, Animated Violence, Realistic Blood & Gore
Resident Evil Survivor	CAPCOM	Mature (17+)	Animated Blood & Gore, Animated Violence
Revelations Series Persona	Atlus Software	Kids To Adults	Mild Animated Violence, Comic Mischief
Revolt	Acclaim	Everyone	Mild Animated Violence
Rhapsody A Musical Adventure	Atlus Co.Ltd	Everyone	Mild Animated Violence
Rising Zan The Samurai Gunman	AGETEC,Inc.	Mature (17+)	Animated Blood, Animated Violence
Rival Schools	CAPCOM	Teen (13+)	Animated Violence
Road Rash 3d	Electronic Arts	Teen (13+)	Realistic Violence, Strong Language, Suggestive Themes
Road Rash Unchained	Electronic Arts	Teen (13+)	Animated Violence, Mild Language
Roadster Trophy	Titus Software - CALIF	Everyone	No Descriptors
Robotron X	Midway Home Entertainment	Teen (13+)	Animated Blood, Animated Violence
Rock the Rink	Electronic Arts	Everyone	Animated Violence, Comic Mischief
Rogue Trip	GT Interactive	Teen (13+)	Animated Violence, Suggestive Themes
Roll Cage	Psygnosis - US	Everyone	No Descriptors
Rollcage Stage II	Psygnosis - US	Everyone	Animated Violence
Romance of the 3 Kingdoms6 Awakening of the Dragon	KOEI Corp.	Everyone	Animated Violence
Rosco McQueen Firefighter Extreme	Psygnosis - US	Everyone	Mild Animated Violence
RPG Maker	AGETEC,Inc.	Everyone	Mild Animated Violence
Rugrats	THQ Inc.	Everyone	Comic Mischief
Rugrats Studio Tour	THQ Inc.	Everyone	No Descriptors
Runabout 2	Hot B USA	Teen (13+)	Animated Violence
Running Wild	989 Studios	Everyone	No Descriptors
Rushdown	Electronic Arts	Everyone	No Descriptors
Saga Frontier	Sony Interactive - Foster City	Teen (13+)	Mild Language
Saga Frontier 2	Square Electronics	Teen (13+)	Mild Animated Violence, Suggestive Themes
Samurai Shodown	Sony Interactive - Foster City	Teen (13+)	Animated Violence, Animated Blood
Samurai Shodown Warriors Rage	SNK Corporation of America	Teen (13+)	Animated Violence
San Fransisco Rush Extreme Racing	Midway Home Entertainment	Everyone	No Descriptors
Scars	Ubi Soft	Everyone	Animated Violence
Scrabble PSX	Hasbro Interactive	Everyone	No Descriptors
SeaDoo Hydrocross	Vatical Entertainment	Everyone	No Descriptors
Sega Ages	Working Design	Kids To Adults	Animated Violence
Sentient	Psygnosis	Teen (13+)	Mild Animated Violence
Sentinel Returns	Psygnosis - US	Everyone	No Descriptors
Shadow Madness	Crave Entertainment	Teen (13+)	Animated Blood, Comic Mischief, Use of Tobacco & Alcohol
Shadow Master	Psygnosis	Teen (13+)	Animated Violence
Shadow Tower	AGETEC,Inc.	Teen (13+)	Animated Violence
Shadowman	Acclaim	Mature (17+)	Animated Blood & Gore, Animated Violence
Shanghai True Valor	Sunsoft	Everyone	No Descriptors
Shaolin	THQ Inc.	Teen (13+)	Animated Violence
Silent Bomber	Bandai America	Teen (13+)	Animated Violence
Silent Hill	Konami USA, Inc.	Mature (17+)	Animated Blood & Gore, Animated Violence
Silhouette Mirage	Working Design	Everyone	Mild Animated Violence, Mild Language
Sim Theme Park	Electronic Arts	Everyone	Comic Mischief
Skullmonkeys	Electronic Arts	Teen (13+)	Comic Mischief, Mild Animated Violence
SlamScape	Viacom New Media	Kids To Adults	Animated Violence
Sled Storm	Electronic Arts	Everyone	Animated Violence
Small Soldiers	Electronic Arts	Teen (13+)	Animated Violence
Sno Cross Championship Racing	Crave Entertainment	Everyone	No Descriptors
Softball Slam	3 DO	Everyone	Comic Mischief
Soul of the Samurai	Konami USA, Inc.	Mature (17+)	Animated Blood, Animated Violence
SoulBlade	Namco Hometek	Teen (13+)	Animated Violence
South Park	Acclaim	Mature (17+)	Comic Mischief, Strong Language
South Park Chef's luv Shack	Acclaim	Mature (17+)	Comic Mischief, Mature Sexual Themes
South Park Rally	Acclaim	Mature (17+)	Comic Mischief, Strong Language
Soviet Strike	Electronic Arts	Teen (13+)	Animated Violence, Realistic Violence
Space Invaders	Activision	Everyone	Animated Violence
Space Jam	Acclaim	Kids To Adults	Mild Animated Violence
Space Station Silicon Valley	Take 2 Interactive Software, Inc.	Everyone	Animated Violence
Spawn the Eternal	Sony Interactive - San Diego	Mature (17+)	Animated Blood & Gore, Animated Violence
Spec Ops	Take 2 Interactive Software, Inc.	Mature (17+)	Animated Blood, Animated Violence
Speed Punks	Sony Computer Entertainment America	Everyone	Mild Animated Violence, Mild Language
Speed Racer	Jaleco	Everyone	No Descriptors
Speedball 2100	Take 2 Interactive Software, Inc.	Everyone	Animated Violence
Speedster or Rush Hour	Psygnosis	Kids To Adults	No Descriptors
Spiceworld	Psygnosis - US	Everyone	No Descriptors
Spider Man	Activision	Everyone	Animated Violence
Spider The Video Game	BMG Interactive	Kids To Adults	Animated Violence, Animated Blood
Spin Jam	Take 2 Interactive Software, Inc.	Everyone	No Descriptors
Sports Car G I	Electronic Arts	Everyone	No Descriptors
Spot Goes To Hollywood	Virgin Interactive	Kids To Adults	No Descriptors
Spyro 2	989 Studios	Everyone	Mild Animated Violence
Spyro the Dragon	989 Studios	Everyone	Comic Mischief
Star Fleet Academy	Interplay Prods.	Kids To Adults	Animated Violence
Star Gladiator	CAPCOM	Teen (13+)	Animated Violence
Star Ocean	989 Studios	Everyone	Animated Violence, Mild Language
Star Trek Invasion	Activision	Everyone	Animated Violence
Star Wars Episode 1 Jedi Power Battles	Lucasarts	Teen (13+)	Animated Violence
Star Wars Episode 1 The Adventure	Lucasarts	Teen (13+)	Animated Violence
Star Wars Master of Teras Kasi	Lucasarts	Teen (13+)	Animated Violence
Steel Harbinger	Mindscape	Mature (17+)	Animated Violence, Animated Blood
Steel Reign	Sony Interactive - San Diego	Teen (13+)	Animated Violence
Streak	GT Interactive	Everyone	No Descriptors

Street Fighter Alpha 2	CAPCOM	Teen (13+)	Animated Violence
Street Fighter Alpha 3	CAPCOM	Teen (13+)	Animated Violence
Street Fighter Collection	CAPCOM	Teen (13+)	Animated Violence
Street Fighter Collection 2	CAPCOM	Teen (13+)	Animated Violence
Street Fighter Ex 2	CAPCOM	Teen (13+)	Animated Blood, Animated Violence
Street Fighter Ex Plus Alpha	CAPCOM	Teen (13+)	Animated Violence
Street Racer	Ubi Soft	Kids To Adults	Animated Violence
Street Sk8er	Electronic Arts	Everyone	Mild Language
Street Sk8er 2	Electronic Arts	Teen (13+)	Mild Language
Strider 2	CAPCOM	Everyone	Animated Violence
Strike Point	American Technos	Kids To Adults	Animated Violence
Striker Pro 2000	Infogrames	Everyone	No Descriptors
Suikoden	Konami USA, Inc.	Kids To Adults	Animated Violence, Mild Language
Suikoden II	Konami USA, Inc.	Teen (13+)	Mild Animated Violence, Suggestive Themes
Super Puzzle Fighter 2 Turbo	CAPCOM	Kids To Adults	Mild Animated Violence
Superbike 2000	Electronic Arts	Everyone	Realistic Violence
SuperCross Circuit	989 Studios	Everyone	No Descriptors
Superman	Titus Software - CALIF	Everyone	Animated Violence
Superman	Interplay Prods.	Everyone	Animated Violence
Surf Riders	Ubi Soft	Everyone	No Descriptors
Swagman	Eidos Interactive (formerly US GOLD)	Kids To Adults	Animated Violence
Sword Blood	Midway Home Entertainment	Teen (13+)	Animated Blood, Animated Violence
Sydney 2000	Eidos Interactive	Everyone	No Descriptors
Syndicate Wars	Origin Systems	Teen (13+)	Animated Violence, Animated Blood
Syphon Filter	989 Studios	Teen (13+)	Animated Blood, Animated Violence
Syphon Filter 2	989 Studios	Mature (17+)	Animated Blood, Animated Violence
T R A G	Sunsoft	Teen (13+)	Animated Violence
Tactics Ogre	Atlus Software	Teen (13+)	Mild Animated Violence, Mild Language
Tai Fu	Activision	Teen (13+)	Animated Blood, Animated Violence
Tail Concerto	Atlus Co.Ltd	Everyone	No Descriptors
Tail of the Sun	Sony Interactive - Foster City	Kids To Adults	Animated Violence
Tales of Destiny	Namco Hometek	Teen (13+)	Mild Animated Violence, Use of Tobacco & Alcohol
Tanarus	Sony Interactive - San Diego	Kids To Adults	Animated Violence
Tarzan	989 Studios	Everyone	Animated Violence
Team Buddies	Psygnosis - US	Everyone	Mild Animated Violence
Team Losi Rc Racer	Fox Interactive	Everyone	No Descriptors
Tecmo's Deception	Tecmo	Teen (13+)	Animated Violence, Animated Blood
Tecmo Stackers	Tecmo	Kids To Adults	Animated Violence
Tecmo Super Bowl	Tecmo	Kids To Adults	No Descriptors
Tekken 2	Namco Hometek	Teen (13+)	Animated Violence, Suggestive Themes
Tekken 3	Namco Hometek	Teen (13+)	Animated Violence
Tempest X	Interplay Prods.	Kids To Adults	No Descriptors
Ten Pin Alley	ASC American Softworks	Kids To Adults	No Descriptors
Tenchu	Activision	Mature (17+)	Animated Blood & Gore, Animated Violence
Tenchu 2	Activision	Mature (17+)	Animated Blood & Gore, Animated Violence
Tennis Arena	Ubi Soft	Kids To Adults	No Descriptors
Test Drive 4	Accolade, Inc.	Kids To Adults	No Descriptors
Test Drive 5	Accolade, Inc.	Everyone	No Descriptors
Test Drive 6	Infogrames	Everyone	Mild Language
Test Drive Cycles	Infogrames	Everyone	No Descriptors
Test Drive Le Mans	Infogrames	Everyone	No Descriptors
Test Drive Offroad	Accolade, Inc.	Kids To Adults	No Descriptors
Test Drive Offroad 2	Accolade, Inc.	Everyone	No Descriptors
Test Drive Offroad 3	Infogrames	Everyone	No Descriptors
Test Drive Rally Michelin Race of Champions	Infogrames	Everyone	No Descriptors
Tetris Plus	Jaleco	Kids To Adults	No Descriptors
The Divide Enemies Within	Viacom New Media	Teen (13+)	Animated Violence
The Fifth Element	Activision	Teen (13+)	Animated Violence
The Granstream Saga	THQ Inc.	Everyone	Animated Violence
The Great Beanstalk	NewKidCo	Everyone	Comic Mischief
The Incredible Hulk The Pantheon Saga	Eidos Interactive (formerly US GOLD)	Kids To Adults	Animated Violence
The Land Before Time Return to the Great Valley	Sound Source Interactive, Inc.	Everyone	No Descriptors
The Lost World Jurassic Park	Electronic Arts	Teen (13+)	Animated Blood & Gore, Animated Violence
The Misadventures of Tron Bonne	CAPCOM	Everyone	Animated Violence
The Need for Speed II	Electronic Arts	Kids To Adults	No Descriptors
The Need for Speed III	Electronic Arts	Everyone	No Descriptors
The Need for Speed V Rally	Electronic Arts	Kids To Adults	No Descriptors
The NHLPA presents Wayne Gretzky's 3D Hockey	Atari Games/Williams	Kids To Adults	Animated Violence
The Smurfs	Infogrames	Everyone	No Descriptors
The Unholy War	Crystal Dynamics	Teen (13+)	Animated Violence
The World is Not Enough	Electronic Arts	Teen (13+)	Animated Violence
The X Files	Fox Interactive	Teen (13+)	Mild Language, Realistic Violence
Theme Hospital	Electronic Arts	Kids To Adults	Comic Mischief
Thousand Arms	Atlus Co.Ltd	Teen (13+)	Mild Animated Violence, Mild Language, Suggestive Themes
Thrasher Skate and Destroy	Take 2 Interactive Software, Inc.	Teen (13+)	Animated Violence
Threads of Fate	Square Electronics	Everyone	Animated Violence, Mild Language
Thrill Kill	Virgin Interactive	Adults Only	Animated Blood & Gore, Animated Violence
Thunder Truck Rally	Psygnosis	Kids To Adults	No Descriptors
ThunderForce V	Working Design	Everyone	Animated Violence
Tiger Woods 99 PGA Tour	Electronic Arts	Everyone	No Descriptors
Tiger Woods PGA Tour 2000	Electronic Arts	Everyone	No Descriptors
Tigger's Honey Hunt	NewKidCo	Everyone	No Descriptors
Time Commando	Activision	Teen (13+)	Animated Violence
Time Crisis	Namco Hometek	Teen (13+)	Animated Violence
Tiny Tank Up Your Arsenal	MGM Interactive	Teen (13+)	Animated Violence, Comic Mischief, Mild Language
TNN Motor Sports Hardcore 2	ASC American Softworks	Kids To Adults	No Descriptors
TNN Motor Sports Hardcore 4x4	ASC American Softworks	Kids To Adults	No Descriptors
TNN Motorsports Hardcore TR	ASC American Softworks	Everyone	No Descriptors
Tobal no 1	Sony Interactive - Foster City	Teen (13+)	Animated Violence
Toca 2 Touring Car Challenge	CODEMASTERS SOFTWARE LIMITED	Everyone	No Descriptors
TOCA Championship Racing	3 DO	Everyone	No Descriptors
Toca Touring Car Championship	CODEMASTERS SOFTWARE LIMITED	Everyone	No Descriptors
Tom Clancy's Rainbow Six	RED STORM ENTERTAINMENT	Teen (13+)	Animated Blood, Animated Violence
Tomb Raider	Eidos Interactive (formerly US GOLD)	Teen (13+)	Animated Blood, Animated Violence
Tomb Raider 2	Eidos Interactive (formerly US GOLD)	Teen (13+)	Animated Blood, Animated Violence
Tomb Raider 3	Eidos Interactive	Teen (13+)	Animated Blood, Animated Violence
Tomb Raider The Last Revelation	Eidos Interactive	Teen (13+)	Animated Blood, Animated Violence
Tomba	Sony Computer Entertainment	Everyone	Comic Mischief
Tomba 2	989 Studios	Everyone	Comic Mischief
Tony Hawk's Pro Skater 2	Activision	Teen (13+)	Mild Animated Violence, Mild Language
Tony Hawk's Pro Skater	Activision	Teen (13+)	Mild Language
Toonenstein "Dare To Scare"	Terraglyph Interactive	Everyone	No Descriptors
Torneko The Last Hope	Enix America Inc.	Everyone	Comic Mischief, Mild Animated Violence
Toy Story 2 Buzz Lightyear to the Rescue	Activision	Everyone	Animated Violence
Trap Gunner	Atlus Software	Teen (13+)	Animated Violence
Treasures of the Deep	Namco Hometek	Teen (13+)	Animated Violence
Trick N Snowboarders	CAPCOM	Everyone	Animated Violence
Triple Play 2000	Electronic Arts	Everyone	No Descriptors
Triple Play 2001	Electronic Arts	Everyone	No Descriptors
Triple Play 98	Electronic Arts	Kids To Adults	No Descriptors
Triple Play 99	Electronic Arts	Everyone	No Descriptors
Tunnel B1	Acclaim	Kids To Adults	Animated Violence
Turbo Prop Racing	Sony Interactive - Foster City	Everyone	No Descriptors
Twisted Metal 2	Sony Interactive - Foster City	Teen (13+)	Animated Violence, Animated Blood
Twisted Metal 3	989 Studios	Teen (13+)	Animated Violence
Twisted Metal 4	989 Studios	Teen (13+)	Animated Violence
Um Jammer lammy	989 Studios	Everyone	Comic Mischief

ESRB Tables • www.esrb.org

181

Uprising	3 DO	Teen (13+)	Animated Blood, Animated Violence
Uprising X	3 DO	Teen (13+)	Animated Violence
Urban Chaos	Eidos Interactive	Mature (17+)	Animated Blood, Animated Violence, Strong Language
V Rally 2	Electronic Arts	Everyone	No Descriptors
Vagrant Story	Square Electronics	Teen (13+)	Animated Violence
Valkyrie Profile	Enix America Inc.	Teen (13+)	Mild Animated Violence, Mild Language, Suggestive Themes
Vampire Hunter D	Jaleco	Mature (17+)	Animated Blood, Animated Violence
Vanark	Jaleco	Teen (13+)	Animated Violence
Vandal Hearts	Konami USA, Inc.	Mature (17+)	Animated Blood & Gore, Animated Violence
Vandal Hearts II	Konami USA, Inc.	Mature (17+)	Animated Blood & Gore, Animated Violence
Vanguard Bandits	Working Design	Teen (13+)	Mild Animated Violence, Mild Language, Suggestive Themes
Vanishing Point	Acclaim	Everyone	No Descriptors
Vegas Games 2000	3 DO	Everyone	Gaming
Vigilante 8	Activision	Teen (13+)	Animated Violence
Vigilante 8 2nd Offense	Activision	Teen (13+)	Animated Violence
Virtual Tennis	Interplay Prods.	Everyone	No Descriptors
Viva Soccer	Interplay Prods.	Everyone	Animated Violence
VMX Racing	Playmates	Kids To Adults	No Descriptors
Vr Baseball 99	Interplay Prods.	Everyone	No Descriptors
VR Football 99	Interplay Prods.	Everyone	No Descriptors
VR Sports Powerboat Racing	Interplay Prods.	Everyone	No Descriptors
Vs	THQ Inc.	Teen (13+)	Animated Violence
Wacky Races	Infogrames	Everyone	No Descriptors
Walt Disney's The Jungle Book Rhythm n Groove	Ubi Soft	Everyone	No Descriptors
Walt Disney World Magical Racing Quest	Eidos Interactive	Everyone	Comic Mischief
War Gods	Midway Home Entertainment	Mature (17+)	Animated Violence, Animated Blood & Gore
Warcraft 2 The Dark Saga	Electronic Arts	Teen (13+)	Animated Blood, Animated Violence
WarGames	MGM Interactive	Teen (13+)	Animated Violence
Warhammer Dark Omen	Electronic Arts	Teen (13+)	Animated Violence
Warpath	Electronic Arts	Teen (13+)	Animated Blood, Animated Violence
WarZone 2100	Eidos Interactive	Teen (13+)	Animated Blood & Gore
Wayne Gretzky's 3d Hockey 98	Midway Home Entertainment	Kids To Adults	No Descriptors
WCW Mayhem	Electronic Arts	Teen (13+)	Animated Violence
WCW Nitro	THQ Inc.	Everyone	Realistic Violence
WCW NWO Thunder	THQ Inc.	Everyone	Animated Violence
WCW Vs The World	THQ Inc.	Kids To Adults	Animated Violence
Wheel of Fortune	Hasbro Interactive	Everyone	No Descriptors
Who Wants To Be A Millionaire	989 Studios	Everyone	No Descriptors
Wild 9	Interplay Prods.	Teen (13+)	Animated Blood, Animated Violence
Wild Arms	Sony Interactive - Foster City	Kids To Adults	Animated Violence
Wild Arms 2	Sony Computer Entertainment America	Everyone	Animated Violence
Wild Thornbury's	Mattel Media INC.	Everyone	No Descriptors
Wipeout 3	Psygnosis	Everyone	Animated Violence
Wipeout XL	Psygnosis	Everyone	Animated Violence
World Cup 98	Electronic Arts	Everyone	No Descriptors
World Destruction League Thunder Tanks	3 DO	Teen (13+)	Animated Violence
Worms Armageddon	Hasbro Interactive	Everyone	Animated Violence
Worms Pinball	Infogrames	Everyone	No Descriptors
Wreckin Crew	Mindscape	Teen (13+)	Mild Animated Violence, Suggestive Themes
Wu Tang Shaolin Style	Activision	Mature (17+)	Animated Blood & Gore, Animated Violence
WWF Attitude	Acclaim	Teen (13+)	Mild Language, Realistic Violence, Suggestive Themes
WWF In Your House	Acclaim	Kids To Adults	Realistic Violence
WWF Smackdown	THQ Inc.	Teen (13+)	Animated Violence, Mature Sexual Themes, Mild Language
WWF War Zone	Acclaim	Teen (13+)	Animated Violence, Mild Language, Suggestive Themes
X Men Mutant Academy	Activision	Teen (13+)	Animated Violence
X Men Vs Street Fighter	CAPCOM	Teen (13+)	Animated Violence
Xena Warrior Princess	989 Studios	Teen (13+)	Animated Blood, Animated Violence
Xena Warrior Princess	Electronic Arts	Teen (13+)	Animated Blood, Animated Violence
Xenogears	Square Electronics	Teen (13+)	Animated Blood, Mild Language, Suggestive Themes
Xevious 3d G Plus	Namco Hometek	Kids To Adults	Mild Animated Violence
You Don T Know Jack	Berkeley Systems	Teen (13+)	Comic Mischief, Strong Language, Suggestive Themes
Youngblood	GT Interactive	Teen (13+)	Animated Blood, Animated Violence

PlayStation 2 Games

Game Title	Publisher	Rating	Descriptor
Army Men Sarge's Heroes 2	3 DO	Teen (13+)	Animated Violence
Disney's Donald Duck Goin Quackers	Ubi Soft	Everyone	Mild Animated Violence
ESPN International Track and Field	Konami USA, Inc.	Everyone	No Descriptors
Gradius 3& 4	Konami USA, Inc.	Everyone	Mild Animated Violence
Madden NFL 2001	Electronic Arts	Everyone	No Descriptors
MOTO GP	Namco Hometek	Everyone	No Descriptors
Ridge Racer V	Namco Hometek	Everyone	No Descriptors
Tekken Tag Tournament	Namco Hometek	Teen (13+)	Animated Violence
The World is Not Enough	Electronic Arts	Teen (13+)	Animated Violence
Walt Disney's The Jungle Book Rhythm n Groove	Ubi Soft	Everyone	No Descriptors
X Squad	Electronic Arts	Teen (13+)	Animated Violence

Additional Resources

The Internet, when used responsibly, is a virtually limitless resource to learn more about games and the gaming world. Here are some tried and true sites we recommend:

www.marspub.com

Mars Publishing's ongoing annex for addenda to this book and all other Parent's Guides. Also features numerous links to many useful Internet sites.

www.esrb.org

The website for the Entertainment Software Ratings Board (ESRB). A complete, searchable, list of rated games (4,000 and growing) as well as ratings for websites and lots of useful information for parents.

Here are some additional Internet sites we recommend:

For game reviews:
Stratos Group	**www.stratosgroup.com**
Games Domain	**www.gamesdomain.com/gdreview**
International Games Network	**www.pc.ign.com**
GameSpot	**www.gamespot.com**

For industry news:
Blue's News	**www.bluesnews.com**
Adrenaline Vault	**www.avault.com**

General game information:
Gone Gold	**www.gonegold.com**
Game FAQs	**www.gamefaqs.com**
GameCenter	**www.gamecenter.com**

NOTES

A *Parent's Guide*™ to
The Internet

The Best Books are from Mars™.

A Parent's Guide™ to

the Internet

A Comprehensive
Guide to
Safe Surfing

Available
SPRING
2001!

MARS
Parent's
GUIDES

MARS
PUBLISHING

Written by **Tom Ono**

The Author

Tom Ono is a writer of books, designer of computer games, and has a background in computer education, both at the K-12 and at the university level. As an educator he has helped design and build courses of multimedia instruction, and grammar school science programs.

S ince the Industrial Revolution, nothing has so much changed the way people work, recreate and communicate as has the Internet. But what does this revolution mean for our children?

Computer education expert and software designer, Tom Ono, discusses what it means to be a parent in an Internet connected world where any information is at our children's fingertips. Tom explores:

- How computers have and will change our schools—kindergarten to college, and beyond.
- Parenting in the Internet connected home.
- The accessibility of digital vice, criminal knowledge and other potentially harmful information.
- The global economy and your child as a target market.

MARS
PUBLISHING